MW01632242

WHERE HAVE YOU GONE '82 BREWERS?

Tom Haudricourt

KCI SPORTS

CREDITS

ISBN: 0-9758769-9-6
ISBN 13: 978-09758769-9-2

This book is available in quantity at special discounts for your group or organization. For further information, contact:

KCI Sports Publishing
3340 Whiting Avenue
Suite 5
Stevens Point, WI 54481
(217) 766-3390
Fax: (715) 344-2668

Publisher: Peter J. Clark
Managing Editor: Molly Voorheis
Photo Editor: Kristofor Hanson
Cover Design: Nicky Mansur
Book Layout and Design: Nicky Mansur
Sales & Marketing: Tim Voorheis
Media & Promotions: Jon Krull, Jason Kalsow

Front Cover Photos: courtesy of courtesy of Milwaukee *Journal Sentinel* and Hank Koshollek and the Madison *Capital Times*

Insert Photos & Backcover Photos: courtesy of Milwaukee Brewers Baseball Club, Milwaukee *Journal Sentinel*, Hank Koshollek and the Madison *Capital Times* and Bob Nelson

Printed and bound by Worzalla Publishing, Stevens Point, WI

DEDICATION

When you're married to a baseball writer, the word you hear most often is "no."

No, I can't go to the movies Friday night. I'm covering the game.

No, we can't go away on Labor Day weekend. I'll be in Pittsburgh.

No, I won't be on time for dinner tonight. The game went 14 innings.

Your wife becomes accustomed to that word. She learns to live with it, but that doesn't mean it's fair. Summer is vacation time for the rest of the working world. Not for those who cover baseball.

So, Trish, sorry about all the times I've said "no." And thanks for saying "yes" 24 years ago.

As for Basil and Brundy, I know I had to cut some of our walks short while writing this book. I'm done now. Go get the leashes.

ACKNOWLEDGEMENT

I didn't start covering the Brewers for the old Milwaukee *Sentinel* until 1985, so I missed their glorious '82 season. In researching that season and the important moments involving each player on the roster, stories from the *Sentinel* and Milwaukee *Journal* proved very helpful. Five years ago, in preparation for the 20th anniversary reunion of that team, the Milwaukee *Journal Sentinel* (the *Journal* and *Sentinel* merged in 1995) published a well-written and enlightening series on the key players and events from that year that also proved useful as background.

Many people involved with the '82 team were kind and generous with their time and memories. Hall of Fame broadcaster Bob Uecker's mental rolodex is amazing, and he eagerly shared stories that made you understand and appreciate what that team was all about. "Ueck" even brokered an interview with one reluctant subject, for which I remain grateful.

Bud Selig, who ran the Brewers from their inception until becoming Commissioner of Baseball on a full-time basis in 1998, has a keen memory and offered stories I'm quite sure never have been printed. Considering his busy schedule, Selig's generosity was not taken for granted.

Dave Nelson, a former Brewers coach and now a team broadcaster and alumni director, assisted in contacting players, and this book would not have been nearly as complete otherwise. Thanks again, Davey.

There were many others who answered questions, provided details and recalled critical events from '82. But, more than anyone else, I must thank the players from that team who so graciously consented to interviews, some in person, others over the telephone. These are their stories, not mine. This is their book. It tells the story of "Harvey's Wallbangers" one more time, in their own words. I can't thank them enough.

FOREWORD

No name is more synonymous with Milwaukee Brewers baseball than Bob Uecker, who began his 37th year in the club's radio broadcast booth in 2007. Known throughout the country as "Mr. Baseball," Uecker was in his 12th season behind the microphone in 1982, the year the Brewers had their most memorable season, advancing to the World Series with a slugging lineup dubbed "Harvey's Wallbangers." The former big-league catcher and Hall of Fame broadcaster grew close to many players on that exciting club and eagerly reminisced about that joyous season in Milwaukee.

*****

Everybody always talks about how close that '82 team was, and there's no question about that. But the No. 1 thing to me about that team was how much talent it had. That was always first. That team won because it had a bunch of really good players. There were Cy Young Award winners, MVPs, future Hall of Famers. It was a lineup in which every guy was capable of hitting a home run or doing something to win a game for you.

The fans loved the players because they were Milwaukee-type guys. They fit right in with the city. The players were accessible and recognizable around town. After games, they'd go over to Ray Jackson's, a great place near County Stadium, and mingle with the crowd. The players would have a beer and talk to fans. Guys were there all the time.

I was around the guys as much as if I were on the team. After games, we'd go out to eat together. We'd play cards — hearts, pluck, whatever. I'd be right in there with the guys, agitating in the clubhouse, like everybody else. I threw batting practice every day. You couldn't help but feel close to them because they were all great guys.

They were really a loose bunch, and they had a lot of fun. Before games, they'd go out on the field and play 'flip.' They'd do that every day. But when the game started, it was all baseball. It seemed like they always felt that somebody on any given day was going to do something to win a game. That's the way they felt. That's the kind of confidence they had, and it's pretty much the way things turned out.

Everybody seemed happy all the time. Sure, guys had some bad days, but for the most part everybody was happy, screwing around, spending time together in the clubhouse, playing tricks on each other. Not that that helps to win, but it sure helps with attitude. It builds camaraderie.

The players would wear coats and ties on the road, but they also had all that hair. A couple of those guys could walk through a door, but their hair wouldn't arrive until five seconds later. If you shut the door too soon, you'd catch their hair. There was a lot of hair on that club. Fu Manchu moustaches, beards. You name it. That was their deal.

The atmosphere in Milwaukee that October was great. It was as good if not better as when the Braves won in 1957. It was such a long period of time between winning, between championships. A lot of people in Milwaukee didn't remember the Braves. By the '82 season, the Brewers had been there a long time. But it had been such a long time since the city won anything. They were really hungry for it, and they loved that team.

In the World Series, I don't have any doubt that the Brewers were the better team. That's not sour grapes because the Cardinals won, and more power to them. But had the Brewers been full-strength, there's no way they lose. Vukie (Pete Vuckovich) was hurt, Rollie (Fingers) was out, (Don) Sutton was out of gas. Had they had a full complement, the Brewers had the better team. The Cardinals had a hell of a Series, and they deserved the championship. But you give me a healthy Brewers team and I'll take my chances.

I guarantee you one thing. Every one of those guys will talk about that particular season and say that was their year. They still talk about it. You don't have many teams like that. That kind of season bonds you together. Those guys will always have that year and the fun they had together.

-Bob Uecker

CONTENTS

INTRODUCTION

Upon setting out to interview 29 players from the Brewers' 1982 World Series club, the first thing that struck me was how many are still involved in baseball, in one form or another.

Seventeen players from that team remain active in the game, be it at the big league level or the minors, professional or amateur, as coaches, instructors, managers, scouts, advisors. You name it. Others were involved at some point in their retirement and could be again if so compelled.

When one considers that 25 years have passed, that's an extraordinary number to still be a part of the game. "We need the money," one former player joked. And, indeed, most of the '82 Brewers retired before the truly big money changed the game (for the worse, some will say).

But it goes beyond merely economic survival. If you don't have something to offer, you're not allowed to hang around. These men still are making their mark, in different ways, from different perspectives.

"I think it says something about their dedication to the game, and how much it meant to them," said longtime Brewers radio voice Bob Uecker, who remains in touch with many players from that '82 team. "A lot of those guys had the opportunity to stay in the game after they finished playing. But you have to be able to teach it, too. Those guys could do that. You sit down and talk to those guys and you realize just how much baseball they know."

It also was immediately evident how vibrant and detailed the memories of that year were to those who played. The passage of time had not dulled the special moments in their minds. Each had distinctly different viewpoints of that season, yet almost to a man, the overriding sentiment was how close those players were. They shared a special bond you don't often see in the game today, a unique and playful camaraderie that continues to connect them to this day.

I am certain each player will enjoy reading what the others had to say about that wonderful summer of 1982. The stories flowed freely, and as one participant noted, some of them might even be true. One certainly would be naïve to think there was no embellishment. But that's the fun of it, right? No two people remember the same event in exactly the same detail.

This book is the first compilation of interviews with every player from the team known as "Harvey's Wallbangers." It was both a challenge and a pleasure to contact each man and open the portal through which their memories flowed.

Twenty-five years have passed, yet Milwaukee baseball fans still openly and willingly express their love for that team. Without hesitation, the former players do likewise for each other. For those who have wondered, "Where Have You Gone, '82 Brewers?" here's the collective answer.

CECIL COOPER

It often has been said that baseball can be a cruel game. But it also can be a game of redemption, a game of second chances. For that matter, third and fourth chances.

Cecil Cooper had that on his mind as he stepped to the plate in the seventh inning of Game 5 of the '82 American League Championship Series against the California Angels. Not only was the veteran first baseman having a miserable day, he was having a miserable series.

Cooper was batting .105 in the series, and he had struck out with two runners on and two outs in the fifth inning. One inning before that, the Gold Glove fielder committed an embarrassing gaffe, scooping up a bunt by California's Bobby Grich and tagging Grich with his mitt while holding the ball in his bare hand. Grich was safe, leading to a run that put the Angels ahead, 3-1.

But now it was a 3-2 game. With two down in the seventh and Charlie Moore on third and Jim Gantner on second, the County Stadium crowd was in full roar. Angels manager Gene Mauch had left-hander Andy Hassler warming up in the bullpen, and the left-handed Cooper fully expected Mauch to come to the mound and remove young right-hander Luis Sanchez.

"I hadn't had a lot of success against Hassler," said Cooper. "I was figuring he was coming in."

In a move that would haunt Mauch and Angels fans for years to come, he stuck with Sanchez. The decision was one strike from paying off when Cooper went with an outside fastball and sent it to the opposite field in left. As Cooper broke out of the box, he watched the flight of the ball and demonstratively thrust his arms downward.

"It was my first thought, to say, 'Get down! Get down!'" recalled Cooper.

The ball did get down, in front of Angels leftfielder Brian Downing. Moore scored and Gantner followed him around, sliding in ahead of the throw to give the Brewers the lead for good and touching off pandemonium in the home dugout and stands.

"That's something I'll never forget, that feeling," said Cooper. "I will always cherish that. It's the biggest moment in my life, from a baseball standpoint. To be able to say I was the guy that got the base hit that put the Brewers in the World Series for their one and only time thus far, that's a big thrill."

With that one dramatic single, arguably the biggest hit in franchise history, Cooper's prior woes were completely erased. Off with the goat's horns. Cooper would be a hero to Brewers fans for life.

"That's why I always say to this day that there was somebody watching over me, bigger than this game, bigger than life itself," he said. "Because I got another chance. Here I am, having a tough day. Not everybody gets another opportunity to get it done. I had failed in almost the same situation, the time before.

"That's the beauty of baseball. If you come through at the end, everybody forgets about what happened before that. Everybody forgot about the messed-up bunt play, the failed opportunity before that. It's 'What have you done for me lately?' I'm grateful I had another chance because it doesn't always work out that way."

Fittingly, the ball was in Cooper's hands when the pennant was clinched. When Robin Yount fielded Rod Carew's smash and fired it to Cooper for the final out of the game, the Brewers were off to St. Louis and a meeting with the Cardinals in the World Series.

To this day, Cooper can't help wondering what might have happened had Mauch summoned Hassler into the game.

"Who knows?" he said. "Mauch probably thought Sanchez was more of a power pitcher and I wasn't really what you'd call a fastball hitter. He has been second-guessed ever since, but that's what this game is all about. It's probably not fair. Hassler could have come in and I'd still get the hit. Or Sanchez could have got me out. He had two strikes on me. Then Mauch looks like a genius."

Unfortunately for Cooper and the Brewers, winning a World Series wasn't meant to be. Milwaukee would go on to lose in heartbreaking fashion in seven games to St. Louis. Seven years earlier, as he was just getting his big-league career going with the Boston Red Sox, Cooper was part of another disheartening Series loss to the Big Red Machine of Cincinnati.

Cooper would get another shot at that ring as bench coach of the Houston Astros, who advanced to the 2005 World Series against the Chicago White Sox. This time, it would be a more methodical beating as the White Sox rolled to a four-game sweep. But no one ever promised story-book endings in the Fall

Classic.

"Still, it was a great experience to be part of three World Series, two as a player and one as a coach," said Cooper. "Most people don't get that many chances. I consider myself very fortunate."

In one of the most lop-sided deals in franchise history, Cooper was acquired from the Red Sox in December 1976 for first baseman George "Boomer" Scott and outfielder Bernie Carbo. Neither Scott nor Carbo would come close to making the impact that Cooper did over the next 10 years in a Brewers uniform. He would quickly emerge as one of the top hitters and run producers in the American League, fitting in nicely in an offensive juggernaut that would come to be known as "Harvey's Wallbangers."

"I give credit to Bud Selig for bringing me to Milwaukee," said Cooper, who still holds the franchise records of 219 hits in 1980 and 126 RBIs in 1983. "He's the guy that gave me an opportunity. It turned out to be a great deal for me and the Brewers. I finally got a chance to be part of something special, be one of the main guys on the team. It helped me grow as a player. It was a wonderful experience."

Making that experience even more special was the manner in which Milwaukee fans accepted Cooper as one of their own. Each time he came to the plate, chants of "Coooop! Coooop!" would rain down from the stands. How many players have their nickname shouted by their fans as a matter of habit? At first, the soft-spoken Cooper didn't know what to make of it.

"That developed over time," he recalled. "The first time I heard it, I actually thought they were booing me. Then I realized they were saying 'Cooop! Cooop!' They would do that all the time. It was pretty special. It shows you how great the Milwaukee fans are. Not many players have that happen. I grew to like those people and I think they grew to like me, too."

Cooper heard those chants throughout the '82 season, during which he batted .313 with a career-high 32 home runs and 121 RBIs. He hit safely in 31 of the last 32 games and led the club with a .365 batting average with men on base. Cooper had a unique hitting style, at least unique to everyone except Rod Carew.

Looking for a hitting approach that worked for him, Cooper grew to like the crouch style employed by Carew, one of the top hitters in the game. Pushing his lanky, 6-foot-2 frame into a low crouch, with his weight back, Cooper would uncoil like a rattle snake and lash out at pitches with a ferocity that piled up the hits. He batted higher than .300 in each of his first seven seasons with the Brewers, topping the 100-RBI mark four times.

"I copied a lot of things from Carew," said Cooper. "You can't do much better than that, when you look at the success he had. I talked to him a lot when I played against him, asked him why he did what he did. I started to emulate it over time. I didn't have that stance when I first came to Milwaukee. I was more upright. I was looking for something that would work for me, and that turned out to be it. When you find something that works, you stay with it."

Off the field, Cooper didn't have to worry about fitting in. The Brewers were a loose bunch who played hard, on and off the field. That camaraderie played a huge role in the team's success, something that Cooper still remembers fondly.

"We had everything, every kind of character you could have," he said. "We had the quiet guys, the vocal guys, the guys that would clown around, the practical jokers, the guys who were real studious. We had all kinds. I fell somewhere in the middle.

"I was the butt of some of those pranks but I didn't do a whole lot of that myself. Gorman (Thomas), 'Vuke' (Pete Vuckovich), (Mike) Caldwell, (Jamie) Easterly, sometimes Ned (Yost) or (Jim) Gantner, those were the guys doing that stuff. I was okay with it because I knew it was all part of being together. The characters were unbelievable."

While many of his '82 teammates were sent packing in the following years or had their careers halted by injuries, Cooper hung on until 1987, when his playing time greatly diminished as the Brewers committed to new first baseman Greg Brock. He hung up his spikes after that season and moved on to a new career as an agent for baseball players. After nine years of negotiating contracts, he got the itch to get back in the game.

In 1997, Brewers general manager Sal Bando, a former teammate, hired Cooper to be the organization's farm director. The challenge of running five levels of a minor league system was too intriguing to turn down, and soon Cooper found himself working for the daughter of his original boss. When Selig became baseball's commissioner, he turned the job of club president over to Wendy Selig-Prieb, who had befriended Cooper during his playing years with the club.

"It's funny how that turned out," said Cooper. "I used to tell Wendy, 'One day you'll run the club and I'll be your farm director.' We used to talk about that all the time. As it turned out, that's exactly what happened. I always thought that would be a job I'd really like, to be able to influence a lot of young players. It's a very challenging job. In my case, it was a little more difficult because I came from the other side. I was dealing with management from the other side of the table. Just like that, I was in charge of about 150 players."

Cooper went on to fill other roles for the Brewers, working as a special assistant to Bando and minor-league hitting instructor. His biggest challenge came in 2002, when he was asked to join the big-league staff as bench coach to interim manager Jerry Royster, after Davey Lopes was fired a couple of weeks into what became the worst season (56-106) in franchise history.

"That was a difficult situation," he said. "I felt somewhat like an outsider. I was kind of from the old regime. Then (general manager) Dean Taylor came in and brought all these new guys in. It wasn't a comfortable setting. The team was doing miserably. So many bad things were happening. We had an interim manager. It wasn't really a good situation, but I tried to make the best of it and learn what the job was about. I think that helped me tremendously."

Next came a two-year assignment as the Brewers' manager at Class AAA Indianapolis. It was there that Cooper got the "fire burning" to be a big-league manager some day. But, as a longtime Houston resident, he couldn't turn down the offer in 2005 to be bench coach for Astros manager Phil Garner, who had piloted the Brewers from 1992-99.

"It was important to get back to Houston because I had kept my home there, even when I was working for the Brewers," said Cooper. "It wasn't an easy thing to do.

"It has been a wonderful opportunity for me. It's a great organization, we have great leadership. I have a real good relationship with Phil. He's very secure in his job. He doesn't have to worry about me. And I'm secure in who I am. It's not a situation where I'm saying, 'I've got to manage.' If it doesn't happen, it doesn't happen. Phil lets you be yourself, and he likes input. That's all you can ask for."

Defining Moment
Delivering the decisive hit in Game 5 of the ALCS vs. California with a two-run single in the seventh: "It's the biggest moment in my life, from a baseball standpoint."

Number to Remember
32 - Home runs during the '82 season, a career high.

Favorite October Memory
Cooper failed in two chances as a player and another as a coach to win a World Series ring but nevertheless said: "I consider myself very fortunate."

NED YOST

The Brewers were preparing for their last road trip of the '82 season, and Ned Yost had no bats to pack.

"All my bats were broken," recalled Yost, a seldom-used backup catcher behind Ted Simmons. "I didn't play much so I didn't order any more."

With the Brewers battling to hold off the Orioles for the American League East Division title, Yost figured he would see little if any action on the final seven-game swing through Boston and Baltimore. Little did he know he'd need a piece of lumber for the biggest at-bat of his life on the second day of that trip.

It was Sept. 29, the second day in Boston. The Brewers had won the series opener, 7-3, to take a three-game lead over the Orioles.

"It was a big game because Baltimore had lost earlier in the day," recalled Yost.

With the score tied, 3-3, in the top of the eighth, Simmons singled with one down. Manager Harvey Kuenn sent speedy reserve outfielder Marshall Edwards in to run for the lumbering catcher, but Red Sox lefty John Tudor eventually worked out of the inning, despite walking the bases loaded.

Just like that, Yost was in the game. He watched from the bench in the top of the ninth as Paul Molitor drew a one-out walk off Red Sox reliever Mark Clear, then swiped second. Clear whiffed Robin Yount for a huge out, bringing the left-handed-hitting Cecil Cooper to the plate.

By that time, Yost figured he'd better find a suitable bat. Rummaging through the bat rack, he settled on a Charlie Moore model. As Yost nervously swung the bat in the on-deck circle, Boston manager Ralph Houk walked to the mound to confer with Clear and catcher Gary Allenson.

was obvious. Who should the right-handed Clear face with the he left-handed Cooper, one of the most dangerous hitters in the Yost, a right-handed reserve with no home runs on the season? didn't have to take Baseball 101 in school to figure that one out. But how, Yost didn't see it coming.

"For some reason, it never occurred to me that they'd walk Coopie with first base open to face me, which was the absolute logical move," said Yost. "I was hoping Coopie would get a hit so I wouldn't have to. Then Allenson comes back and sticks his arm out (for the intentional walk). I say, 'Oh, crap.'

"Now, I start figuring out how I'm going to win this game. My best thought, against Mark Clear, who had one of the best breaking balls in the American League, was to try to hit a blooper to right field. That's all I could think of."

Sure enough, Clear threw a first-pitch curve that buckled at Yost's knees. The pitch broke over the plate but fooled umpire George Maloney, who called it ball one. Boos rained down from the Fenway Park faithful, and Yost backed out of the box in amazement.

"I thought, 'How could the ump miss that?'" said Yost. "I was totally over-matched."

Perhaps flustered by the call, Clear came back with a fastball, right down the middle. Yost put his best swing on it, and the ball sailed off on a high arc toward the Green Monster. Boston leftfielder Jim Rice looked up and started fading back toward the warning track.

"Everything went into slow motion," recalled Yost. "I'm thinking, 'Oh, Lord, don't catch it.'"

There would be no catching this ball. Not only did it clear the Monster, it sailed over the netting on top and into the dark of the night. Incredibly, Yost had just smacked a three-run homer, his first of the year, to propel the Brewers to a 6-3 victory.

With no practice whatsoever on his home-run trot, Yost sped around the bases. When he got back to the tiny visiting dugout, it was pandemonium.

"There was a lot of pounding, a lot of slapping on the back," said Yost. "It was kind of a madhouse. We looked up and Harvey had kind of fallen down between the bat rack and bench. It was a mess. They were helping Harvey up. It was pretty exciting."

The improbable victory put the Brewers on top of the division by four games with five to play, a seemingly safe cushion. There was no way to predict they would lose the next four games, including the first three in Baltimore, to force a do-or-die showdown on the last day of the season. The Brewers would pull out that final game to win the division, making Yost's dramatic blast all the more important in retrospect.

"It was by far the highlight of my career," said Yost. "I think everybody is meant to have one thing to hang on to and be proud of."

Yost would never have another such moment in the spotlight. After seeing only 61 games of action with the Brewers in 1983, he was traded to the Texas Rangers for catcher Jim Sundberg. By the end of 1985, after a brief stay with the Montreal Expos, Yost was out of the majors for good.

But, beginning with that huge home run in Boston, Yost's baseball experience just got better and better. Though he didn't play in the stunning ALCS victory over the California Angels, Yost will never forget counting down the outs in Game 5 at County Stadium after Cooper's dramatic two-run single put the Brewers on top, 4-3, in the seventh inning.

"When it got down to the last three outs, the place was going absolutely nuts," said Yost. "When it got down to one out in the ninth, I'm in my own little world in the bullpen, thinking, 'One out to the World Series!' Then I hear over the PA: 'Now batting for the California Angels, No. 29, Rod Carew.' My heart just sunk. I'm thinking, 'My gosh, we've got the best hitter in the American League and a runner on second.'

"Then Pete Ladd threw the pitch and Carew hit a one-hopper right to Robin at short. It was smoked but Robin caught the ball, took a step and when he threw the ball to first, he raised his arms right away. I saw it and started jumping up and down. Before the ball even got to Cooper, I had jumped the fence

Fans stormed the field following the Brewers defeat of the California Angels propelling the Brew Crew to their first-ever World Series.

and was sprinting to the mound.

"I wanted to be in that pile. Back then, everybody jumped on the field. I'm on the pile with my teammates and all of a sudden we got crushed by a wave of people. I literally could not move. I was with Sal (Bando) and Paul. We were hugging. I couldn't even move my feet. I said, 'I'm going down, I'm going down!' Sal said, 'Don't go down.'

"All of a sudden, Robin kind of cleared a hole. We got behind him and made it about halfway to the dugout. Then we got sucked in again. By the time I got to the dugout, I was exhausted. I had never been through anything like that. Then we went upstairs and the celebration began again. It was pretty wild."

As exhilarating as that experience was, Yost remembers the utter devastation of losing Game 7 of the World Series in St. Louis. The Brewers were leading, 3-1, heading into the bottom of the sixth, but the game slipped away in the final innings, leaving everyone in a Milwaukee uniform with an empty feeling.

"When we took the lead, at that point in my life, I was the most excited I've ever been," said Yost, who appeared only in the Game 6 blow-out by the Cardinals. "I've never been so excited in my life.

"Then, they take the lead back. That was the absolute worst I've ever felt in my life. You can imagine the gamut of emotions I went through. Not even when my kids were born did I feel that. I had gone from the most excited I had ever been in my entire life to feeling as bad as I've ever felt, in the course of a half hour. That's the beauty of the World Series.

"After the game, it was bad. Guys were crying. They had played their hearts out."

After being released by Montreal in '85, Yost figured his playing days were done. He returned home to contemplate what to do next with his life. Then, one day, he walked in the door and his wife, Deborah, told him he had missed a telephone call.

"She said, 'Somebody named Hank Aaron called for you,'" Yost recalled. "I said, 'Yeah, right. Hank Aaron called for me.' I figured it was one of my friends playing a joke on me. The next day the phone rings again and I answered it and it was Hank. He was Atlanta's farm director and they had some pitching prospects at Double-A and they wanted a veteran catcher. They wanted to know if I'd be interested in being a player/coach. I said, 'What else am I going to do? If I don't like it, I can always go home.' I went and that turned my career around."

Yost bounced back and forth between Class AA Greenville and Class AAA Richmond for a couple of years, then decided the player/coach thing had run its course. The Braves offered him the manager's job at Class A Sumter, which seemed like something he should try. After two years there, an old Brewers teammate came calling. Ted Simmons, then running the St. Louis Cardinals' farm system, called the Braves to ask permission to offer Yost a job managing his Double-A club.

Before talking to Simmons, Yost was asked to place a call to Bobby Cox, Atlanta's general manager at the time.

"I had known Bobby, and he liked me," said Yost. "He said, 'Ned, the Cardinals have called and asked permission to talk to you. It's a great job, I'm not going to lie to you. But I just want to let you know next year there could be some major changes in this organization. If you choose to stay here, you could very well be in the middle of some of those changes.' I said, 'Bobby, that's all I need to hear. Call St. Louis and tell them I don't want to talk to them.'"

Feeling bad about turning down Simmons' offer, Yost placed a call to his former teammate a few weeks later. Simmons immediately put him at ease for deciding to stay with the Braves.

"He said, 'I just wanted to make sure they loved you. If they didn't love you, I was going to bring you over here. But it looks like they love you,'" recalled Yost. "Teddy always looked out for me."

True to his promise, Cox became the Braves' manager the next year and invited Yost to join his staff as bullpen coach. It was the beginning of a 12-year run for Yost with Atlanta, during which the club evolved into the class of the National League.

Yost doesn't hesitate to list the three biggest influences on his life and career — Simmons, Cox and late NASCAR legend Dale Earnhardt. Yost became a close friend of Earnhardt's and even spent a few races in his pit crew, serving as "re-hydration engineer," a fancy racing term for water boy.

"Dale Earnhardt taught me how to compete," said Yost. "Bobby Cox taught me how to manage and treat people. And Ted Simmons taught me the game."

Those lessons from Simmons were imparted on a daily basis when they played together with the Brewers. It astonished Yost at the time that the savvy veteran would take the time to share his wisdom and knowledge with a raw, seldom-used backup catcher.

"He came up to me one day and said, 'I want to see you tomorrow morning at 7 o'clock,'" said Yost. "I went home thinking, 'What did I do?' I hadn't really ever talked to Teddy. I ran to look to see if anybody put his glove in my locker and he thought maybe I stole it. What could it be?

"The next day at 7 o'clock, I'm sitting there in my uniform. Teddy came in like he usually does, with his cigarettes, gets dressed and comes over and sits down. He says, 'I've been in this game a long time. I've had a lot of people take the time to sit down and teach me this game. I want to do the same for you. Every day, I'm going to have something for you, and we're going to sit and talk about it.'

"Every single day for the next two years, Ted Simmons had something to talk about. We'd talk before the game, after the game. It involved hours a day. I grew to love it. He taught me things I had never thought about."

Thanks to that guidance from Simmons, Cox and Earnhardt, Yost found himself in position to be considered for the Brewers' managerial opening after the 2002 season. It was initially offered to Oakland's Ken Macha, which devastated Yost, but Macha turned it down and fate once again intervened.

After an absence of nearly 20 years, Yost was back in a Brewers uniform. It was his dream job, an opportunity that far exceeded merely being a manager in the big leagues.

"I always knew in my heart, my first job would be manager of the Milwaukee Brewers. Deborah and I always said that," said Yost, who helped the Brewers snap a 12-year losing streak with an 81-81 record in 2005. "I didn't care about being 'a manager.' That didn't really cut it with me. It all revolves back to '82. I wanted to be the Brewers manager because I wanted to bring that excitement and that passion the city has for the team back to Milwaukee.

"People think that's hokey, but that's a huge part of what I live for. We're not there yet but we're definitely headed in the right direction."

Defining Moment

Socking the game-winning homer in Boston on September 29, giving the Brewers a four-game lead with five to play: "It was by far the highlight of my career."

Number to Remember

1 - Homer hit by Yost in 1982, but it was a huge one.

Favorite October Memory

Jumping on the pile of players after beating California in Game 5 of the ALCS at County Stadium: "I had never been through anything like that."

PETE VUCKOVICH

By his own admission, Pete Vuckovich has lived with the guilt for 25 years. It's a guilt the 1982 Cy Young Award winner never should have carried, according to his teammates.

When Vuckovich took the mound for the Brewers in Game 7 of the World Series in St. Louis, it was the final step of what had been a childhood dream. Growing up in Johnstown, Pennsylvania, the rugged pitcher of Serbian descent decided it was his destiny to be on baseball's biggest stage at some point.

"It's a day you simulate as a young pitcher, whether you're throwing a ball off the wall or whatever," said Vuckovich. "It's the game you dream about your whole life. It's the game you dream of going out and dominating and helping your team be world champions."

And for five innings, with the entire baseball world looking on, things were going according to plan for the man his teammates called "Vuke." After the Cardinals scored in the fourth inning, Brewers left fielder Ben Oglivie tied the game with his first post-season home run, off of Joaquin Andujar.

The Brewers then went on top, 3-1, with two runs in the sixth. Andujar's throwing error on Paul Molitor's bunt set up the first run, and Cecil Cooper delivered the other with a sacrifice fly. To that point, Vuckovich had been in typical form, pitching in and out of trouble, never conceding, stranding runners and doing whatever it took to keep St. Louis off the board.

But things began to unravel in the bottom of the sixth. With one down, Ozzie Smith singled and raced to third when Lonnie Smith followed with a double. Manager Harvey Kuenn, knowing Vuckovich was pitching with a battered shoulder and basically getting by on guile, decided it was time to go to his bullpen, and summoned lefty Bob McClure.

McClure found more trouble by walking Gene Tenace to load the bases, then surrendered a base hit up the middle to Keith Hernandez that tied the game. George Hendrick followed with an RBI single, delivering what proved to be the winning run. The Cardinals would tack on two more runs in the eighth en route to a 6-3 victory that completed the comeback from a three-games-to-two hole.

Afterward, in the somber visiting clubhouse of Busch Stadium, Vuckovich was devastated. He couldn't get past the idea that he had let down his teammates, that they had counted on him to win Game 7 and he couldn't deliver.

"You go out there, it's the seventh game, you have the opportunity to go nine, shut them down and win," said Vuckovich. "I failed to do that and I've carried that burden ever since 1982. All these years, I've felt guilty for letting my teammates down. It's that simple."

Never mind that Vuckovich was pitching with what later was discovered to be a torn rotator cuff in his shoulder, the most dreaded of injuries for pitchers. He was running on fumes in September and had little left in the post-season, when he failed to win either of his two starts in both the ALCS against California and the World Series.

"Vukie pitched anyway, but his arm was blown," said catcher Ted Simmons, who knew exactly what his closest friend had to do to mask the pain before each start. "He wouldn't quit. He kept going out there and trying to help his team win.

"The game has changed in many ways since then. There's a more conservative approach to rehabilitation, and all those sophisticated things that go on now, with insurance purposes, etc. That wasn't done back then. Guys went out and pitched."

No matter what it took, at least in the case of Vuckovich. It was no secret in the clubhouse that Vuckovich took pain injections in his shoulder before many of his starts. And if that particular shot didn't do the trick, he'd ask for another. He didn't see it as heroism or recklessness or any of the above. He merely felt it was his duty to take the mound and do whatever it took to help the Brewers win a game.

"Teddy and I would talk about it all the time," said Vuckovich. "We would say, 'There's no correlation between how you feel and what you accomplish. It doesn't matter.' Physically, I might not have been as capable as I wanted to be, but mentally I felt I was strong enough and knew enough about my trade and craft to take care of business.

"I failed to do that and I've lived with that ever since. I know I had their respect. That's fine, that's nice. I just personally felt I let them down. I was driven as a pitcher. I was competitive. I had goals. I had a goal at that point in time to win the seventh game of the World Series. I failed and I've had to live with it. I've always felt shitty about that."

Perhaps, but without Vuckovich's contributions, the Brewers never would have been playing that October. He won 18 of 24 decisions, pitched nine complete games and reeled off two eight-game winning streaks, the second of which came down the stretch run when every victory was critical.

With 234 hits and 102 walks in 223 2/3 innings, Vuckovich became accustomed to pitching from the stretch. He refused to give in to hitters, working deep into counts without fear. Vuckovich also tried every trick in the book to distract hitters. He was in constant motion on the mound, going into all sorts of gyrations, constantly twitching and flinching, jerking his head from side to side.

It was not uncommon for Vuckovich to walk behind the mound, bend over and dry heave. Wearing a uniform that seemed two sizes too big, sporting a sinister Fu Manchu moustache and peering at hitters from under a cap pulled low, the 6-4, 220-pound Vuckovich was an intimidating presence on the mound.

"He tried to create distractions," said Simmons, who came with Vuckovich and closer Rollie Fingers from St. Louis in the December 1980 trade that put the Brewers on the path to the World Series. "Whether it's a Mark Fidrych or somebody else, everybody's got their shtick. Not everybody can back their shtick up. Peter could do that.

"You can't fake it out there. You have to have the stuff, too. He just tried to get an edge, whatever it might be. Peter was always looking for an edge, and he usually got it because he had talent. You have to have that first."

That talent was sorely tested in the second half of the season as Vuckovich's shoulder began to unravel. Some pitchers would have asked to go on the disabled list. But Vuckovich plugged along, in large part due to his love for manager Harvey Kuenn, who took over the sputtering club in early June when Buck Rodgers was dismissed.

"It could be said I gave up my career for Harvey Kuenn," said Vuckovich. "I probably pitched more than I should have. But he had an awful lot to do with that. He walked around on one leg. He was as game as any man I ever met in my life, and it kind of rubs off on you."

Asked if he might have prolonged his career by easing off the pedal a bit in '82, Vuckovich said, "I have no idea, nor do I care. I would never do that to Harvey or my teammates. Those guys were plugging away. That team was driven, that team wanted it and went after it.

"A lot of guys were playing hurt. How many guys had surgery after that season? You don't talk about those things. That's a built-in excuse. You go out and compete. We went out there and tried to beat you, whether we were physically capable or not. You could feel great and have a bad day or feel terrible and have a good day. It was a matter of being there for your teammates."

The following spring, it was discovered just how much damage Vuckovich did to his shoulder by continuing to pitch. He eschewed surgery to repair the torn rotator cuff, pitched in only three games that season and missed all of '84. For all intents and purposes, his playing career was over.

Forced into retirement after pitching in only six games in 1986, Vuckovich looked for ways to stay in the game. For three years, he worked as an analyst on the Brewers' television broadcasts. Vuckovich had a face for radio but put his vast knowledge of the game to good use in that role. In typical self-deprecating style, he now makes fun of that brief TV career.

"I failed at that, also," he said. "It's totally different. You're removed from the game itself. I enjoyed it, but I guess I wasn't good enough. After the third year, one writer said it was an oxymoron for Pete Vuckovich to be a broadcaster. I said, 'Why did you call me a moron?' I didn't know the meaning of oxymoron. It's different from being in uniform."

Vuckovich did wear a major league uniform one last time in 1989, but it was the pinstripes of the New York Yankees. He took a memorable acting turn in the baseball movie *Major League*, deftly playing the role of menacing slugger Clue Haywood.

In 1992, Vuckovich's former battery mate and close friend, Simmons, was hired to be the Pittsburgh Pirates' general manager. He offered Vuckovich a job as the Pirates' minor-league pitching instructor, a position the former ace hoped in vain he'd get offered by the Brewers one day.

"That's one of the more disappointing things," he admitted. "I did want to be a Milwaukee Brewer forever. It's the best organization I've played for. It was the first time I played in a city and bought a home there. I lived there for 11 years, raised my family there. I never did that in any of the other cities I played in.

"I wanted to be a Brewer forever and it didn't work out, unfortunately. You'd have to ask the people in charge there why. I guess I wasn't good enough. I loved the city, I loved the people. I was part of the Brew Crew. It just didn't work out."

After Simmons left Pittsburgh to recover from a heart attack, Vuckovich remained in the organization. He eventually worked his way up to special assistant to the general manager, a role in which his scouting acumen and player evaluation talents were evident.

"This may sound stupid, but I'm more proud of [his current role] than I am that I was a big-league pitcher," said Vuckovich. "I didn't know if baseball would deem me worthy enough to stay in the game after I was through pitching. I wasn't the nicest guy. I did have a bit of a reputation. You often wonder if baseball permits guys like that to stay in the game.

"I expected to be a pitcher in the big leagues. I didn't expect to stay there afterward. This is what I know. This is what I love. I'll do whatever baseball wants me to do. I think I'm versatile enough and know the game well enough to do whatever they want me to do."

Defining Moment
Winning the 1982 Cy Young Award after leading the Brewers with 18 victories.

Number to Remember
30 - Starts made in 1982 despite an ailing shoulder that got worse as the season progressed.

Favorite October Memory
For Vuckovich, who went winless, there was none: "All these years, I've felt guilty for letting my teammates down."

DWIGHT BERNARD

Dwight Bernard isn't sure why he went missing in the fall of 1982.

Bernard had been a key component of the bullpen for the Brewers throughout the season, ranking second on the club with 47 appearances. He compiled a 1.62 ERA in his first 20 outings after Harvey Kuenn took over as manager on June 2. Yet, as the season wore down, he was used less and less. And once the Brewers advanced to the playoffs, he barely took off his warm-up jacket.

"Down the stretch, I got some saves when Rollie (Fingers) was hurt," said Bernard. "Then, they stopped using me. I don't know why. A lot of guys were saying, 'Are you all right? Are you hurt?' I was fine. The big reason was (pitching coach) Pat Dobson. That was his doing."

Bernard had pitched twice in the 1981 Eastern Division mini-playoff series against the New York Yankees, without yielding as much as one hit. Yet, in the '82 ALCS against California, he was given just one inning of action, mopping up at the end of the 8-3 loss in Game 1 in Anaheim.

Bernard wasn't used again that October until Game 6 of the World Series, closing the final inning of a dreadful, rainy 13-1 pounding in St. Louis. He turned in another hitless inning, and it certainly beat not getting to pitch at all in the Fall Classic. But it wasn't exactly the way Bernard envisioned things unfolding.

"It was disappointing," he admitted. "I thought I'd see more action. But at least I can say I pitched in the World Series."

Getting to that World Series was easier said than done. The Brewers had to win in Baltimore on the final day of the season to win the AL East and avoid a historic collapse, then rallied from a 0-2 hole in the best-of-five ALCS against the Angels.

"They were chirping in the papers out there," Bernard said, referring to the very confident Angels. "They thought they had us.

"Everybody was tired when we got out there. We had been on the road a long time, then went across the country. Once we got back home, it made a big difference. We got back to Milwaukee early in the morning and the airport was packed with fans. It was unbelievable. Everybody just kept playing. We just said, 'Keep doing what you've done all year.'"

The Brewers came close to winning it all despite the loss of Fingers to an elbow injury. Down the stretch, the bullpen was in a state of flux, with starting pitchers such as Moose Haas and Bob McClure getting relief assignments and rookie Pete Ladd seeing action as the closer. By October, Bernard had become lost in the shuffle.

"I think we all thought we were going to win when we went back to St. Louis (for Games 6 and 7)," Bernard said. "I just wish I'd had a better chance to pitch. Who knows? I might not have gotten anybody out. We've talked about that for years. We did it one way all year and then changed it. I don't know why."

Few things came easy for Bernard, who had to survive eight seasons in the minors before finally getting the call from the Brewers near the end of the strike-shortened split season in '81. A second-round draft pick in 1974 by the New York Mets, the Illinois native was acquired by Milwaukee after the '79 season in a trade for pitcher Mark Bomback.

After that one inning in the '82 World Series, Bernard would never pitch in the major leagues again. He was released by the Brewers near the end of training camp the next spring, a move that stunned him.

"I couldn't believe it," he said. "Rollie came up to me and said, 'What's wrong with you?' When I showed him the (release) paper, he said, 'You've got to be kidding me.' Then Don Sutton saw it and went and made a phone call. He got me a job. I went to Houston (Sutton's former club) immediately.

"That year, they started moving guys [to other teams]. They started making changes. It happened pretty fast. It became a different team."

Bernard kicked around in Houston's farm system for a couple of years, then pitched in Double-A for Baltimore. The writing was clearly on the wall. He wasn't going to make it back to the big leagues. It was time to get on with the next phase of his life. Still dedicated to his craft, Bernard decided he might have a career as a pitching coach.

"I never thought about it when I was playing," said Bernard. "I was still throwing in the low 90's (mph) when I quit. I hadn't thought much about coaching."

Once he decided to go that route, Bernard dived in and didn't look back. He coached for a year in Pittsburgh's system, then began a seven-year hitch coaching minor-league pitchers for Minnesota. After working in the Alaskan Summer League in 1997, Bernard finally found his way back to the Brewers.

For six years, Bernard coached in the Brewers' system. He started at Class AA El Paso, then jumped to AAA and coached at Louisville and Indianapolis. Midway through the 2002 season, Brewers bullpen coach Bill Castro was named interim pitching coach after Dave Stewart left that troubled club. Bernard was promoted to the majors to assume Castro's original duties in the bullpen. The next season, he was re-assigned as Milwaukee's minor league pitching coordinator.

"It's fun to see when those kids move up," said Bernard. "That's your reward. It was good to get back with the Brewers. I had Ben Sheets down there, Jeff D'Amico, guys like that. Those guys were pretty good pitchers. You knew Ben would move up and be a good one. When he's healthy, he's as good as they come."

After the 2003 season, the Brewers "decided to go a different way," as Bernard recalled. He went back on the job market and was hired by the Seattle Mariners. Again, he bounced around, coaching at Class A Inland Empire, Class AA San Antonio and Class AAA Tacoma, where he is today.

"I was sad to leave the Brewers, but I like it here," he said. "I've moved up every year. I've written a manual on pitching mechanics, some things that I used myself. I've been in the game 34 years. I never could have imagined that."

As a youngster growing up in Mount Vernon, Illinois, Bernard adopted the Cardinals as his favorite team. He found it more than a bit ironic that he was pitching for the Brewers years later when they squared off against St. Louis for all the marbles. He didn't get a ring that fall but did pick one up in 1987, and again in 1991, by coaching in Minnesota's system in the years in which the Twins won World Series crowns.

"So, I have two World Series rings and one American League championship ring," said Bernard, a recent inductee into the Mount Vernon High School athletic Hall of Fame. "That's not too bad."

As for his short but memorable tenure with the Brewers, Bernard will never forget what the team did on the field in '82, even if it ended in personal disappointment over his reduced role and professional disappointment over losing the World Series. For good reason, he said that clubhouse had a sense of confidence you don't find with ordinary teams.

"Every time you took the field, every time you walked on that mound, you knew you had a chance to win," he said. "There was that winning atmosphere, that winning feeling. It was always there. If you came in and did your job, you knew you were going to win. That was something special.

"If we lost a game, we'd forget about it, go out early the next day and play 'flip.' We were never too tight to have fun. That's the way it was all year. There weren't many losing streaks. Off the field, we'd go out together; it might be 15 guys. At home, guys had parties that everybody went to. The guys liked being with each other. We hung out all the time. You don't see that anymore."

Defining Moment
Helping the Brewers make their move under new manager Harvey Kuenn, with a 1.62 ERA over his next 20 appearances.

Number to Remember
6 - Saves in '82, tied with Jim Slaton for second-most behind Rollie Fingers (29).

Favorite October Memory
With only two post-season appearances, there weren't many. "At least I can say I pitched in the World Series."

MIKE CALDWELL

Some pitchers live in mortal fear of folding under pressure. Others fear the possibility of a career-ending injury.

Mike Caldwell feared running out of ketchup.

Like most businessmen, but unlike most baseball players, Caldwell carried a briefcase with him wherever he went. In it, you would find only one item: a bottle of ketchup. Actually, that's not true. Sometimes the crafty left-hander would have two bottles of ketchup in the briefcase.

"What can I say? I love ketchup," explained Caldwell. "Hotels never gave you enough, so I carried it with me everywhere. I read an article once that said some lady in Russia lived to be 114, and she mentioned ketchup as the one thing she ate all her life. So, I thought I'd stick with it."

During spring training, Caldwell and catcher Ted Simmons lived in the same complex and often carpooled to the ballpark in Sun City, Arizona. One morning, when Simmons was doing the driving, Caldwell reached into a bag and pulled out a can of asparagus. Then, he opened his briefcase and took out his ketchup bottle. Caldwell opened the can, pulled out a stalk of asparagus, coated it with ketchup and gobbled it down.

As the astonished Simmons looked on, Caldwell finished off the entire can in that fashion.

"It was 8 o'clock in the morning," Simmons recalled with a laugh. "I thought I was going to puke. I said, 'Why are you trying to provoke me, man?' He said, 'I'm not. It's good this way.' Mike put ketchup on everything he ate. I mean everything. He had to have it. I don't know how to explain it. Does that make him unusual? I suppose. But that doesn't make him a bad person, right?"

Caldwell might have had his quirks off the field, but on a pitching mound he didn't mess around. He quickly developed into a big-time winner for the Brewers, going 22-9 in his first full season with the club in 1978.

The Brewers had acquired Caldwell from Cincinnati in the middle of the '78 season, pulling off one of the biggest steals in franchise history. To get Caldwell, the Brewers surrendered two minor leaguers, left-hander Rick O'Keefe, the club's 1975 first-round draft pick, and outfielder Gary Pyka. If you haven't heard of them, that's because neither played a day in the major leagues.

"The deal that brought Caldwell from Cincinnati was some kind of deal," said longtime Brewers radio voice Bob Uecker. "I don't know why they didn't like him in Cincinnati. Nobody gives up a 20-game winner if they can help it. O'Keefe was supposed to be a big-time prospect, but he never did anything. It turned out to be a hell of a deal."

By the start of the 1982 season, Caldwell had established himself as one of the top pitchers in the American League. In his first four full seasons with the Brewers, he compiled a 62-35 record. That trend continued in '82, as the North Carolina native crafted a 17-13 record with 12 complete games and three shutouts. The Brewers scored a mere 23 runs in his 13 losses.

With a bushy mustache, what seemed like three or four days growth of beard, a baggy uniform and a penchant for being in the middle of clubhouse pranks, Caldwell fit in nicely in a very loose organization.

"I was right in the middle of it," he recalled. "I was getting jokes played on me as fast as I could pull them on other guys. I always thought if you were the recipient of a prank, someone cared enough about you to do it. They got out of hand at times but nothing too serious."

If you played a prank on a teammate, you knew there would be retribution at some point. Once, after Simmons had worked feverishly to properly align the colors on a Rubik's Cube, Caldwell sneaked it away and "unaligned" it. The next day, as the Brewers prepared to leave Texas and head home, Caldwell's clothes were missing from his locker.

"I found my whole suit in the hot tub," said Caldwell. "Teddy did it because I messed up his Rubik's Cube. It was travel day and my suit, my shoes, everything I was going to wear home was in the hot tub, soaking wet. I had to wear my uniform home. Luckily, we were on a charter. You get a little pissed at first, then you say, 'Don't get mad, get even.'"

No player was immune from those hi-jinks. Closer Rollie Fingers, the 1981 AL MVP and Cy Young Award winner, learned to hide his car keys or pay the price.

"We used to take Styrofoam cups and stick a pen in there and hang Rollie's keys in a cup of water," said Caldwell. "We'd put them in a freezer for a few hours and then put them in his locker at the end of the game."

Caldwell was at his best in the heat of the pennant race, going 10-1 with a 2.20 ERA and seven complete games from July 31 to September 22. After the

Caldwell celebrates after completing a dominant three-hit shutout as the Brewers won Game 1 of the '82 World Series 10-0 over the Cardinals.

Brewers finally clinched the AL East title in Baltimore on the last day of the season, Caldwell was given the Game 1 assignment in the ALCS against the California Angels in Anaheim. He couldn't deliver, surrendering six runs in three innings in an 8-3 defeat.

The Brewers also dropped Game 2 and headed home to Milwaukee, down two games to none in the best-of-five series. It was a deficit from which no major league club had escaped.

"I don't remember ever thinking we were going to lose," said Caldwell. "Even coming back on the plane from California, we were upset and knew how hard a thing we had to do, but after we won the first game, I don't think there was a doubt that we could win that series."

And the Brewers did exactly that, winning three in a row at home to advance to the World Series against St. Louis. Caldwell got the ball in Game 1 once again, and this time he didn't disappoint. In fact, Caldwell completely dominated the Cardinals, pitching a three-hit shutout as the Brewers steam-rolled the NL champs in a 10-0 victory.

The Cardinals were a speedy team that put the ball in play and kept pressure on the opposing defense, but they were no match for Caldwell's nasty sinker. They grounded into 14 infield outs, playing pepper throughout the night with second baseman Jim Gantner, who had seven assists.

"I think the Cardinals were trying to do the thing they wanted against me," said Caldwell. "They were trying to do the correct thing against a guy who was going to throw a lot of sinkers. They just happened to hit balls right at people.

"To be perfectly honest, I felt no pressure. I had pitched fairly poorly in Game 1 of the ALCS against the Angels. Then we had the audacity to come back and beat them to get into the World Series. For me, Game 1 was a bonus. It was like, 'Wow, here I am. I'm going to go out and pitch like I pitch.' I kept the ball down and things went very well for us.

"The guys played great defense behind me. Every pitcher on that staff knew one thing — if we went out there and pitched, didn't give up a lot of runs, and kept the game fairly close, we had a good chance to win because we had some offense and a fairly solid defense."

Caldwell took the mound again in the crucial Game 5, with the World Series even at two games apiece. The winner would be one victory away from the title, and with the last two games in St. Louis, the Brewers considered it a must-win situation. This time, the Cardinals didn't hit every ball at a defender. Caldwell found himself pitching from the stretch all day, thanks to surrendering 14 hits in 8 1/3 innings. But he refused to cave in, and the Brewers pulled out a 6-4 nail-biter.

"That, for me, was one I was more proud of pitching than the three-hit shutout," he said. "I gave up 14 hits and still came within one double-play ball of pitching a complete game. There were men on base the whole damn game. I got outs when I needed them. Charlie Moore made a great play in that game in right field. Cecil Cooper made a diving play at first base. It was a tremendous ball game.

"We had played all year just to get to that point. I always felt energy from the crowds in Milwaukee. I always wanted to pitch well for them. It's a blue-collar, beer-drinking, hard-working town. They were great fans, not the totally obnoxious fans of New York and Philly, but very knowledgeable fans. They had been following baseball for years. They always felt a little outcast because the Braves had left them."

Alas, a World Series title was not meant to be for the Brewers, who dropped the last two games in St. Louis. Much like the team itself, Caldwell began to slip after that season, winning only 12 games in 1983 and going 6-13 the following season, his last in the big leagues. Caldwell returned home to Raleigh, North Carolina, and finished his sociology degree at N.C. State, figuring he was done with baseball.

When the head coaching job at Campbell University was offered to Caldwell a few years later, he decided to get back in the game. He stayed there for five years before deciding to return to the pro ranks. What prompted that change? "The NCAA manual," he said. "It went from being the size of a program to a phone book. I was kind of missing pro ball. I made a couple phone calls to the Brewers and was able to get a job with them."

Caldwell served as a pitching coach and manager at several stops in Milwaukee's farm system, including the rookie ball club in Helena, Montana, Class A High Desert in California, Class AA Huntsville and Class AAA Indianapolis. After a gig as Indy's pitching coach in 2004, however, he was not invited back for another season.

"I very much enjoyed being a minor league coach with the Brewers," said Caldwell. "I might still be there but (farm director) Reid Nichols didn't like what I was doing, so he fired me."

He latched on with Detroit's farm system, coaching pitchers at Class AA Erie for three years. Before the 2007 season, he was hired by the San Francisco Giants to be the pitching coach for Class AAA Fresno. Caldwell was interviewed for this book near the end of Fresno's training camp in Scottsdale, Arizona. Earlier that morning, he had begun to pack his car for the drive to California. As usual, he made sure one item in particular was safely tucked away for the trip.

"I just packed my briefcase this morning," he said. "There's no ketchup in it, but there's a bottle in another box. I had two in my room. I only used one."

Defining Moment
Blanking St. Louis on three hits in Game 1 of the World Series: "To be perfectly honest, I felt no pressure."

Number to Remember
12 - Complete games pitched en route to leading the club with 258 innings pitched.

Favorite October Memory
Winning Game 5 of the World Series despite allowing 14 hits in 8 1/3 innings: "I got outs when I needed them."

DON MONEY

In his prime, Don Money was one of the top defensive third basemen in the major leagues. Before his playing days were done, he held fielding records in both leagues, once going 257 chances without committing an error.

By the time the '82 season rolled around, however, Money was near the end of his distinguished career. He had played 14 years in the majors, including nine with the Brewers — the longest tenure of any player in club history at that point — and would turn 35 that summer.

With the Brewers committed to young, exciting third baseman Paul Molitor, Money found himself in a platoon at designated hitter with another veteran, Roy Howell. The right-handed-hitting Money played against lefties and the left-handed-hitting Howell against righties. Money would get an occasional start at third base or first, but for the most part his value came with a bat in his hands.

"I took ground balls every day (during batting practice), but I only played a handful of games in the field," he recalled. "My last four or five years, that's basically what I did. I could still swing the bat a little. Roy and I knew our roles, and we got along fine. DH-ing was tough at first because you really have to set your mind on it. You hit, then you sit down. You don't play the other half of the game. It's different."

Actually, Money could swing the bat more than "a little." In 96 games that season, the four-time all-star batted .284 with 16 home runs and 55 RBIs, impressive totals considering he had only 275 at-bats. Yet, the Brewers' lineup was so formidable that manager Harvey Kuenn put Money and Howell in the No. 7 spot for most of the season.

"That team could hit," said Money. "One thing we didn't have any trouble doing was scoring runs. That was a pretty strong lineup."

With a roster full of strong personalities. Players had to keep their wits about them, on and off the field, fending off pranksters in the clubhouse and participating in cut-throat 'flip' games before batting practice. During 'flip,' players formed a circle and batted a baseball at each other with their gloves, using enough force to cause fat lips, bloody noses and other assorted wounds. If you weren't able to keep the ball in play, you dropped out of the circle.

"I bet we had 20 guys playing 'flip' most days," recalled Money. "And I mean hours upon hours. I remember we were in Seattle in the old [Kingdome]. We'd catch cabs to the park about 2 o'clock, get dressed and go out and play 'flip.' We'd go into the right-field corner and play 'flip' for about three hours.

"It was fun. It kept everybody loose. Nobody really got hurt. I know today they don't want guys doing it. I understand that. In Yankee Stadium, they had that low fence. We'd be right there in the corner playing, and the fans would come down and watch. Nobody wanted to be the first guy out."

Most of the players came early, and many stayed late. Long after games were over, they would remain in the clubhouse, drinking beer, playing cards or just shooting the bull. On the road, no one was anxious to go back to the hotel.

"Today, they have Nintendo games and all that in the clubhouse," said Money. "Sometimes, we didn't even have a TV. We'd sit in the clubhouse and have a beer and talk about the game. Or we'd say, 'Let's go to Joe's Bar and have a beer.' We'd walk in, six, seven, eight of us. Then we'd listen to each other talk about ball. I'd ask a pitcher what he was thinking when he threw a certain pitch. You'd want to hear what the pitchers were thinking because then maybe you'd look for the same pitch in that situation when you were hitting.

"You don't see that anymore. After games, guys come in and eat, then go their different ways. Things have changed. Our after-game meal would be a tub of cheddar cheese. We'd have crackers to dip in it. And we'd have beer or soda. Now, they have big meals. They have food before games, too. I couldn't eat before a game. I liked to have an empty stomach when I played. I couldn't have all that stuff in my stomach."

Money was a clutch performer throughout the '82 season, batting .345 with runners in scoring position, with a career-best .531 slugging percentage. He didn't make much impact in the post-season, however, batting .182 in the ALCS against California and .231 in the discouraging seven-game World Series loss to St. Louis. But there was one personal family highlight in the Fall Classic. In the first two games at Busch Stadium, Money's 12-year-old son, Don Jr., served as one of the batboys.

"I asked Sully (equipment manager Bob Sullivan) where the batboys came from on the road," recalled Money. "He said the home team supplied them. I asked him if it would be all right if my son did it and he said yeah. We got some pictures of him doing it. I told him, 'It took me 14 years to get to the

World Series and it only took you 12."

Though the Money-Howell platoon worked well, the Brewers began using catcher Ted Simmons in the DH role in 1983. Money began spending more time on the bench, getting only 114 at-bats and responding with a .149 batting average.

"I hit the ball hard but didn't get any hits," he said. "That's baseball."

After the season, general manager Harry Dalton asked Money if he'd be interested in playing in Japan. The Kintetsu Buffaloes were willing to pay the Brewers for Money's services, and Dalton told him he no longer was in the club's plans. At age 36, Money decided "what the heck," so he packed up wife Sharon and their two children and headed for Japan. A short time later, he decided he had made a big mistake to become a gaijin (imported player).

"I came home after three months," said Money. "I had enough of that. It just wasn't for me, the way things unfolded. I had to take three different trains every day to the ballpark. The money wasn't what they said it was going to be.

"I wasn't used to their style of play. I'm watching our team make an error or strike out with a man on third base. They walk back and act like nothing happened. I stood up and yelled, 'Let's show some emotion some time.' It just didn't pan out."

Money returned home to Vineland, New Jersey, and spent time with his family, something a ball player rarely gets to do. He kept his hand in the game by coaching at Sacred Heart, the local Catholic high school. Don Jr., who went to the public school, Vineland High, squared off against his dad's team a couple of times each year, providing talk for the dinner table.

"We were the second-smallest school in New Jersey," recalled Money. "The graduating class was only 50 or 60 kids. I enjoyed it. The only thing I had a problem with was we didn't have a field. We had to use the city park. You had to be off the field at a certain time. We had some pretty good teams. We got beat in the state finals once and in the second round once."

Money also coached a semi-pro team, but it just wasn't the same as his days with the Brewers. Once his children were grown and out of the house, he placed a call to former teammate Cecil Cooper, who was running the Brewers' farm system.

"I'd like to get back into baseball. Do you have any openings?" Money asked.

Cooper told Money he was reorganizing his minor league staff and would get back to him. Sure enough, he called a few weeks later and offered Money the managing job with the Brewers' rookie-ball club in Helena. But Money never made it to Montana.

"I was at a charity golf tournament in Princeton, N.J.," recalled Money. "I walked in the house and my wife said 'Coop called.' I said, 'Does he want me to manage in Beloit?' She said, 'Yeah, how did you guess that?' I had read he needed a manager there."

So, Money went back to the Midwest, managing at Class A Beloit, just over an hour down the road from Milwaukee. He stayed there seven years, a prolonged assignment that might have caused some ex-big leaguers to chafe. But Money enjoyed working with the younger players in the system, imparting knowledge accrued during his long career.

"I had the opportunity to leave a couple of times, but I stayed there," he said. "I didn't mind it. As a matter of fact, I loved working with kids in their first full season. You try to lay the ground work for them to become a professional. They had never played a 140-game season. I told them, 'You're going to do something you've never done before and you'll never do again — play your first 140-game schedule.' That's a long season when you're not used to it. You could see the guys run out of gas at the end."

Three years ago, Money accepted the opportunity to manage the Brewers' Class AA affiliate in Huntsville, Alabama. He moved up a rung on the organizational ladder, and might find himself running the club at Class AAA Nashville some day, and who knows after that? At this point, he's taking things as they come.

"I enjoy it," said Money. "My No. 1 goal is not to get back to the big leagues. I've been there. Yes, if they called me up and said they wanted me to come up there, that would be fine. That's where it's at. That's where we're trying to get all these guys. But if it doesn't happen, that's fine, too. My job is to get these players ready to go to the next level.

"We have our ups and downs, like everybody. We have a few long bus trips. It's not too bad. If you don't like your job, it'll show."

Defining Moment

Played his 10th season as a Brewer in '82, at the time a club record.

Number to Remember

Money batted .345 with runners in scoring position during the 1982 season.

Favorite October Memory

Playing in his first World Series game and contributing a run-scoring single in the Brewers' 10-0 victory in the opener in St. Louis.

DON SUTTON

As soon as Don Sutton arrived in the visitors' clubhouse at Memorial Stadium, he sought out Brewers trainer John Adam.

"I don't want to alarm anybody, but I'm starting to feel a little run down," Sutton told Adam. "Do you think the doctor can give me an injection?"

For as long as the veteran right-hander could remember, a shot of penicillin had done the trick every time he felt a bug coming on. It was the final weekend of the season, and if the Brewers won either game of the make-up doubleheader on Friday against Baltimore or the game Saturday afternoon, Sutton would be saved for Game 1 of the American League Championship Series.

Just to play it safe, Sutton figured he'd better engage in a bit of preventative medicine.

The Orioles' team doctor was summoned but wasn't too keen on the injection idea. But he was assured by Sutton that the pitcher was not allergic to penicillin, and finally relented.

"He filled my butt with penicillin," recalled Sutton, who stayed in the clubhouse while the Brewers went out and were bludgeoned in both ends of the doubleheader, 8-3 and 7-1, despite having their top starters, Pete Vuckovich and Mike Caldwell, on the mound. When Sutton awoke the next morning in his room at the Cross Keys Inn, he was sweating and feverish. He pulled up his T-shirt and discovered red blotches all over his abdomen. In a mini-panic, Sutton rushed to the ballpark and slipped into the trainer's room without letting on he was in trouble.

Sutton walked up to Adam and said, "If I was to have a reaction to medicine, how would I know it?" Before the trainer could answer, Sutton lifted up his shirt. Adam's jaw dropped.

"He was covered with welts — red, angry-looking welts," recalled Adam. "I'm thinking, 'We're all in trouble now.'"

Adam made another call to the Orioles' doctor, who administered another injection, this time cortisone. "Good luck," said the doc before disappearing out the back door of the trainer's room. As the Brewers took the field, Sutton remained behind, soaking in a whirlpool of cool water.

Making matters worse, Baltimore spanked the Brewers again, 11-3, drawing into a tie for first place in the AL East. Milwaukee had blown all of its three-game lead and now faced a win-or-go-home game with the reinvigorated Orioles on the final day of the season. There would be no saving Sutton for the playoffs now. He would have to pitch the biggest game in the history of the franchise, welts or no welts.

"I was preparing to celebrate on Saturday or pitch on Sunday," said Sutton, who never let manager Harvey Kuenn know about the penicillin debacle. "Either way, it would have been fine. It wasn't that big of a deal."

Sutton even accompanied a group of players that evening to Baltimore's Little Italy, where former third baseman Sal Bando, now an unofficial coach and assistant to general manager Harry Dalton, was hosting a dinner.

"I wasn't going to miss Bando picking up a check," recalled Sutton with a laugh. "Are you crazy? I would have taken an ambulance to that. We had dinner and it was great. Everybody was fine, loosey-goosey. I didn't get a sense that anybody was 'puckered.'"

That mood might have changed had Sutton revealed his allergic reaction to the penicillin shot. Wisely, he figured what his teammates didn't know wouldn't hurt them.

"I had a couple of glasses of wine and a nice dinner, then went back to the hotel and slept like a baby," said Sutton.

The next morning, when Sutton walked into the visiting clubhouse, he made eye contact with a very nervous Adam, who had not slept nearly as well. Sutton gave a thumbs-up, and Adam almost melted onto the floor in sheer relief.

Sutton walked over and whispered to Adam, "I'm going to pitch my ass off and win this game."

It was Sutton's reputation as a big-game pitcher that prompted Dalton to acquire him from Houston on August 30, one day before the deadline to retain post-season eligibility. Dalton surrendered outfield prospect Kevin Bass and pitchers Frank DiPino and Mike Madden, but he thought the price was well worth getting another experienced arm for a thin rotation.

At 37, Sutton's best days were behind him, but he still knew a thing or two about pitching. He won three consecutive decisions entering the finals series in Baltimore, giving the Brewers just the lift they needed. Now, matched up against Orioles ace Jim Palmer, Sutton had his new club's season squarely on his shoulders.

"I wasn't scared; I wasn't nervous," he recalled. "I honestly felt like, 'What a privilege it was to have the ball that day.' The organization had killed itself all year to get to that point. I got on at the last stop. At that time, I considered it the biggest game of my career. It was a responsibility, and I love responsibility."

The morning of the game, Sutton was sitting alone in the hotel restaurant, eating breakfast and reading the newspaper. He felt somebody slip into the other side of the booth and looked up to see none other than legendary broadcaster Howard Cosell, who would be working the game that afternoon.

"How are you, Don?" Cosell said in his booming baritone voice.

"I'm fine, Howard," responded Sutton.

"Are you nervous?" asked Cosell.

"No, I'm not nervous," replied Sutton.

"How does it feel to be pitching against Palmer in the big game?" said Cosell, continuing his inquisition.

"Why don't you ask Jim how it feels to go against me in the big game?" said Sutton.

Cosell bellowed with laughter, fully enjoying the repartee. But Sutton wanted some peace and quiet and asked Cosell to leave. The Mouth that Roared did so, grudgingly.

Sutton reported to the ballpark, took off his clothes and went to the trainer's room to get tape jobs on his left heel and right big toe. Sutton had been plagued by blisters on those areas and routinely was taped before taking the mound. As Adam worked on Sutton's feet, shortstop Robin Yount stuck his head in the door.

"The veins in his neck were bulging and his eyes were real big," recalled Sutton. He said, 'Don't make us have to score five to get even and we'll kick [Palmer's] ass.' That wasn't like Robin. He was usually soft spoken. It showed how much it meant to him."

Yount certainly did his part, socking homers off Palmer in his first two at-bats. Cecil Cooper and Ted Simmons also went deep, and Ben Oglivie made a rally-killing catch in the left-field corner in the bottom of the eighth. Given that support, Sutton worked around eight hits and five walks to hold the Orioles to two runs in eight innings.

Sutton had done exactly what he was acquired to do — pitch the Brewers into the post-season. A monumental collapse had been averted, and the newly-crowned AL East champs were soon jetting across the country to California to begin the ALCS against the Angels.

"It was an awesome day," said Sutton. "That ranks among my top three thrills ever in sports."

As it turned out, Sutton had one more season-saving start in him. After the Brewers lost the first two games in California, he got the ball in Game 3 when the team finally returned home to County Stadium. Sutton held the Angels at bay for 7 2/3 innings, the Brewers squeezed out a 5-3 victory and they were on their way to a miraculous come-from-behind triumph in the series, something no team previously had done in the best-of-five format.

"Winning Game 3 put the pressure squarely on them," said Sutton. "Had it turned out different, I might feel differently now. But I would have felt disadvantaged if I didn't have that opportunity. I never guaranteed success. I just told Harvey, 'Give me the ball and I'll give you all I've got.'

"The atmosphere was unbelievable. Sunday, when we won (Game 5), you couldn't drive down the streets. I was staying in a hotel downtown and I walked from the ballpark to the hotel. People were everywhere."

Unfortunately for the Brewers, Sutton was pitched-out when they advanced to the World Series to play St. Louis. He had worked 54 2/3 innings in seven starts since coming from Houston, an average of almost eight innings per outing. Prior to the trade, he accumulated 195 innings in 27 starts. Toss in the ALCS outing and the odometer on Sutton's arm registered 257 1/3 innings, his heaviest workload in six years. Sutton even warmed up in the bullpen near the end of Game 5 of the ALCS in the event he was needed to stave off elimination one more time.

"I wasn't 25 years old," he said. "When I got to St. Louis, I was out of gas. If I wasn't out of gas, the tank was awfully low. There wasn't a whole lot left. That's why I've always said I wish I could have given Milwaukee 'younger innings' in the World Series. It would have been fun."

Sutton allowed four runs in six innings in Game 2, which St. Louis won, 5-4. It got even uglier in Game 6 as he was pummeled for seven runs (five earned) in 4 1/3 innings in a 13-1 thumping that allowed the Cardinals to pull even in the Series, setting up their Game 7 triumph.

Including three World Series with the Los Angeles Dodgers, Sutton was 0-for-4 in his quest for a ring. He stumbled to an 8-13 record in 1983, when a late fade signaled the beginning of the end of the Brewers' glory days. He bounced back with 14 victories in '84 but it was evident he had no place in what became a rebuilding plan for the club.

Sutton was 39, and he yearned to end his career back home in California. He hoped for a deal to the Angels, who played 18 miles from his home in Laguna Hills. Instead, he was traded to Oakland, a destination so undesirable that Sutton reported 14 days late to spring training after threatening to retire. As it turned out, he fit right in, compiling a 13-8 record before the Athletics shipped him to California, the team he hoped to join all along.

Sutton won his 300th career game in 1986 and made one last trip to the playoffs with the Angels. After one more season with California, he came full circle and signed with the Dodgers, his original team. It turned out to be a bad idea, and he was released in August, putting an end to his career.

"It wasn't a smart move to go back to LA," he recalled. "I was going through some personal issues at home at the time. I turned down a lot of money to go to Japan. You can't go home. I knew that was going to be my last year, and I thought it was the right thing to do. It would have been easy to go to Japan and take the money and run."

Sutton had done some work in radio and television during various off-seasons, including a gig as a country music disc jockey. Thus, it made perfect sense to move into the broadcasting side of baseball, and he soon landed what would become an 18-year stint with the Turner Broadcasting System, doing telecasts and radio broadcasts for the Atlanta Braves.

"It was the perfect fit for me," said Sutton, who finished his 23-year career with a 324-256 record and 3,574 strikeouts. "I'm from Alabama, I grew up in Pensacola, and I've got relatives from Atlanta to Mobile. That's the one job I wanted. I was doing a pre-game show for the Dodgers that first year and I lived on Delta, going back and forth across the country. But I loved every minute of it. I had talked with (Braves broadcaster) Pete Van Wieren years before and I told him, 'Some day you and I arc going to work together.' To this day, we still talk about that conversation."

Sutton's life soon took more dramatic turns. He remarried, and in 1997 wife Mary gave birth to a daughter, Jackie, who was born 16 weeks early and weighed only 19 ounces. Given little chance to survive, Jackie proved to be a fighter and fooled the doctors.

"She's my miracle, absolute miracle," said Sutton, who now makes his home in Rancho Mirage, California. "We were going to neonatal intensive care, twice a day, for 129 days. One day I walked out of the hospital and a guy from a TV station said, 'You didn't make it.' I didn't even know what he was talking about. All I had on my mind was my little girl."

Sutton had failed for the fourth time to be elected to the Baseball Hall of Fame. But the fifth time was the charm. In 1998, he was inducted, and daughter Jackie was mentioned prominently in his acceptance speech.

"I said something like, 'Little girl, thanks for sticking around to be a part of it,'" recalled Sutton, getting a bit choked up at the memory. "We take her every year to Cooperstown. Really, she has grown up there."

Now in his first year doing TV broadcasts of Washington Nationals games for the Mid-Atlantic Sports Network, Sutton still looks back on the final month and a half of the '82 season with great fondness.

"I can't think of another six weeks in my career that meant as much to me and still does as my six weeks in Milwaukee," he said. "If you're a person who takes pride in your work like I did, you can't script it any better than those six weeks. The only thing that would have made it better was to win the World Series.

"That's the most amazing collection of players I've ever been around. We had two altar boys, four guys that looked like they had just escaped from Attica state prison, and 19 of us somewhere in the middle. It was an amazing group. We would go down together, fighting together."

Defining Moment

Pitching the Brewers to a 10-2 victory in Baltimore on the final day of the '82 season, clinching the AL East crown in a do-or-die game: "That ranks among my top three thrills ever in sports."

Number to Remember

Sutton went 4-1 in seven starts with the Brewers after being acquired from Houston in '82.

Favorite October Memory

Winning Game 3 of the ALCS against California, beginning the Brewers' stunning comeback from a 0-2 deficit in the best-of-five series.

GORMAN THOMAS

It not only was the saddest day of Gorman Thomas' career, it was the saddest day of his life.

The Brewers' slugging center fielder was relaxing at home on June 6, 1983, when his telephone rang. General manager Harry Dalton was calling to tell Thomas he had been traded to Cleveland.

"What?" said Thomas, who made Dalton repeat the news to make sure he heard correctly.

Dalton gave Thomas no reason for the trade that sent the ultimate fan favorite to the Indians with reliever Jamie Easterly and minor league pitcher Ernie Camacho for center fielder Rick Manning and pitcher Rick Waits. Thomas put down the telephone and cried.

"I was stunned, devastated," he recalled. "I never saw it coming. I don't know why I was traded. I know unequivocally that I never did anything that was inappropriate. Sure, they were getting somebody (in Manning) who could run faster but that was it.

"That ruined the rest of my career. It became just a job. I still played hard but it was just a job. I wanted to be in Milwaukee."

Yes, Thomas was struggling mightily at the plate that season, batting .183 with five homers and 18 RBIs through 46 games. But the year before, he slugged 39 homers and drove in 112 runs, helping the Brewers make it to their first World Series. Over the previous five seasons, Thomas had sent 175 pitches over the fences, the highest total of any player in the American League.

Thomas had been with the Brewers from the very beginning, before they were even the Brewers. He was a first-round draft pick in 1969 by the Seattle Pilots, a doomed club that existed for only one season before being bought out of bankruptcy and moved to Milwaukee. Thomas debuted in the majors in 1973, playing on some truly dreadful teams until the Brewers finally started winning five years later.

"The first few years, we did well to win 60 games," he recalled. "We had a few quality players, but no one of superstar stature. The team wasn't to the point where we could get to the promised land."

That changed in 1978 with the arrival of manager George Bamberger. The Brewers won 93 and 95 games, respectively, in Bambi's first two seasons, but that wasn't good enough to make the playoffs in the ultra-competitive AL East. Still, the Brewers had turned the corner. They made it to the mini-playoffs in the strike-split season of 1981, setting the stage for their big breakthrough the following year.

"We played in the best division in baseball, at that point in time," said Thomas. "All the pieces were there, but we just couldn't get over that last hump. Then, in '82, it happened."

Finally pushed over the top by the blockbuster trade that brought starter Pete Vuckovich, closer Rollie Fingers and catcher Ted Simmons from St. Louis in December 1980, the Brewers were positioned to make their push. When Harvey Kuenn replaced manager Buck Rodgers on June 2, the '82 team took off.

Thomas was an all-or-nothing hitter prone to strikeouts (he led the AL in 1979 and 1980) but also capable of going on prolific home-run binges. A career .225 hitter, Thomas' offensive game was power and run production. In the field, Thomas was hardly the prototype center fielder. He had little speed to speak of but would give up his body to make a catch, crashing into walls and eating lots of grass while making diving stabs.

That take-no-prisoners style of play made Thomas a fan favorite among blue-collar Milwaukee fans, leading to his nickname, "Stormin' Gorman." He furthered that bond by frequenting tailgate parties in the parking lots around County Stadium, both before and after games.

"I'd show up for an afternoon game and the tailgating would be going on," he said. "I'd have a Coke and a brat. Then, I'd come back after the game and have a beer. It was no big deal. Some of the other guys did it.

"The fans liked me because I played hard. I knew what it meant to get a chance. I waited a long time, and I wasn't going to let it be taken away from me. I played to the best of my ability every moment. I played with reckless abandon. It wasn't something I thought about. It was just the way I was taught."

"Hitting home runs is what I did. I didn't hit .300. (Pitching coach) Cal McLish called me over one day and said, 'Gorman, all I want you to do is catch the ball and take care of my pitchers. Just play hard and you'll earn their respect.'"

Thomas received hitting tips from teammate Don Money, a sweet-swinging veteran who never had trouble making contact with pitches. Money told Thomas to stop flailing at high fastballs he couldn't reach and start looking for the sliders that pitchers used to bury him.

"So, basically, that's what I did," said Thomas. "Except for obvious 2-0 or 3-1 counts, I looked for the slider. That's why I hit as many homers as I did.

"In center, I made up for what I lacked in speed with intelligence. I knew my pitchers and I knew the opposing hitters. I knew my ballpark, and I got a good jump on the ball. I was a good center fielder. I thought I was underappreciated as far as my defense went, though when I was playing, I didn't say that because you don't toot your own horn."

Off the field, Thomas often could be found in the middle of the action in a clubhouse full of pranksters. He kept his teammates loose with his Southern drawl and knack for story telling, most of which would make a sailor blush. One thing you didn't want to do: turn your back on Thomas when he was in a devilish mood.

"If you give, you were going to get," he said. "There was no doubt about that. You're a target no matter what because you were going to get blamed for it."

Thomas and Vuckovich hit it off immediately, and over time they became inseparable. They teamed up to pull pranks on teammates in the clubhouse, and they hit the bars together after games. Vuckovich called Thomas "Spike," a nickname that made the rounds on the club.

"We were kind of alike," said Thomas. "When we got between the lines, it was 'play hard.' Off the field, we had fun together. We thought pretty much the same way."

A few years later, when Thomas was playing in Seattle, he got a telephone call from the injury-ravaged Vuckovich, who was trying to keep his career alive in Milwaukee at the time.

"Spike, send me a thousand dollars," said Vuckovich.

"Are you all right?" replied Thomas.

"Yeah, just send me a thousand dollars," said Vuckovich.

Thomas put a check in the mail and didn't hear another word from his buddy for a couple of weeks. Vuckovich called again, asking for another thousand bucks, still without explanation, and Thomas dutifully mailed another check.

A month later, Vuckovich called once again, asking for two thousand dollars. This time, Thomas wanted details.

"I ain't sending you another penny until you tell me what's going on," said Thomas.

"We bought a bar," said Vuckovich.

"Really? What's the name?" asked Thomas.

"Stormin' and Vuke's," replied Vuckovich.

"It was over in the south side of Milwaukee," said Thomas. "It had been an old Serbian meat market. Vukie had a bunch of his gumbahs help out and fix the place up. It turned out pretty good. But I was only in it for about a year before I got out."

When Thomas flips through his mental rolodex of the '82 season, he often focuses on the final weekend in Baltimore, when the Brewers dropped the first three games to set up a winner-take-all finale. The night before that memorable last-day victory over the Orioles, Thomas looked out his hotel window to see team owner Bud Selig walking back and forth in the courtyard.

"That was back when he was smoking Tiparillos," recalled Thomas. "He was out there pacing, in front of the shops, in front of the restaurant. Just watching him do that, I said to myself, 'Bud, you better get some sleep. We've got a big game tomorrow.' The next day, Robin (Yount) hit two home runs, I took a home run away from Ken Singleton and Benji (Oglivie) made that catch in left field (of an opposite-field drive by Joe Nolan). That particular day is always the first thing that comes to my mind."

The Brewers pulled off a miraculous comeback against California in the ALCS and came within a game of beating St. Louis in the World Series, but that October was not a time of personal joy for Thomas. He tore up a knee sliding home in Game 3 against the Angels and batted only .067 in that series, with one homer. Still hobbled against the Cardinals, he hit a mere .115 with no homers.

"You didn't think about injuries," he said. "You just went out and played. You figured if you didn't, you were letting your teammates down. Vukie had a 104-degree fever in the last game of the World Series (not to mention a torn rotator cuff). You wanted to be in the lineup."

Thomas has watched replays of the final out of that World Series ad nauseum. He swings and misses at a high fastball from St. Louis closer Bruce Sutter, touching off a red-clad celebration at Busch Stadium.

"They don't show that I fouled off six pitches before that, against one of the best relievers in the history of the game," said Thomas. "And the score was 6-3. It would have been different if it was a one-run game or somebody was on base. It was a high fastball, too, of all things. I kept fouling off his splitter, so he threw one up there. It happens.

"After the game was over, I don't remember much. I do remember getting on the charter and sitting in the very back with Robin. We were having a beer, and both of us were crying. To get that close and not get it was tough. You look at it and you say, 'This might be the only time ever.' And it was."

More shocking than the loss to the Cardinals was how quickly that team was dismantled. Thomas was one of the first to go, a move that many of his teammates insist to this day tore the heart out of the team.

Gorman Thomas slides into Angels catcher Bob Boone in Game 3 of the 1982 American League Championship Series. Thomas ended up hurting his knee on the play but gamely played on in the rest of the ALCS and World Series.

"To me, the trade of Gorman took one of the corks out of our bottle," said Mike Caldwell, the crafty lefty who won both of his World Series starts. "There was nothing wrong with 'Archie' Manning. It added more speed in center field. But Gorman was part of us. It was like one of our lungs or kidneys was missing. We all missed Gorman. It's like taking a '65 Mustang and turning it into a '95 Mustang. It's the same car, but it ain't the same."

Thomas actually was traded twice by the Brewers. He was sent to Texas after the 1977 season to complete an earlier trade but was purchased from the Rangers before the start of spring training in '78. The second time, there was no reversing the deal.

Dalton tried to put the genie back in the bottle in the second half of the 1986 season when he re-signed Thomas, who had been released by Seattle. But there was no magic left in Thomas' bat, and he called it a career after batting .179 with six homers and 10 RBIs in 44 games with the Brewers. Going through a divorce at the time, Thomas turned down an offer to play in Japan.

After retiring, Thomas returned to his hometown of Charleston, South

Carolina, spending most of his time on golf courses and fishing boats. He has played on various celebrity golf tours but nothing made him happier than when the Brewers summoned him back to their family in 1995. Thomas accepted a scouting assignment in Greenville, South Carolina, where the ACC baseball tournament was played.

"I saw about 16 games in three days," he said. "I enjoyed it. I saw a lot of good players. I sent my report in. But that was my last scouting assignment."

Club president Wendy Selig-Prieb had another venture in mind for one of her favorite former players. A dining area dubbed "Gorman's Grill" opened at County Stadium, and Thomas was invited back to serve as host. He has retained residence in the Milwaukee area ever since, remarrying and doing all manner of personal services for the club. "Gorman's Grill" was transformed to "Gorman's Corner" when Miller Park opened in 2001.

"It's flattering to have something like that with your name on it," he said. "I'm on the payroll. I go certain places and do certain things, representing the club. I love it. I consider myself a Brewer."

Thomas, who has been inducted into both the South Carolina and Wisconsin Halls of Fame, hoped the Brewers eventually would get around to offering him a coaching job, but it never happened. He still can be found at the ball park during most home stands, mingling with players, fans and media. The game retains that undeniable tug on a former player considered the very soul of "Harvey's Wallbangers."

"I love coming to the ballpark," he said. "I come out as much as I can. I like being in the clubhouse and out on the field, talking to the players. I just enjoy being around baseball."

Reflecting back on that glorious summer of 1982, he added, "I find it hard to believe it's been 25 years. People still talk about that team, and rightfully so. Guys used to get fed up hearing everybody talk about the '82 team. But, you know what, we were a winner. We didn't win it all, but we were a winner."

Defining Moment

Striking out against St. Louis closer Bruce Sutter to end the World Series: "They don't show that I fouled off six pitches before that, against one of the best relievers in the history of the game."

Number to Remember

Thomas hit 175 home runs from 1978 through 1982, the most of any player in the American League.

Favorite October Memory

Capping a six-run rally in the seventh inning with a two-run single as the Brewers rallied to win Game 4 of the World Series, 7-5, at County Stadium.

TED SIMMONS

Ted Simmons had the right to nix the trade. After spending more than 10 years in St. Louis, where he made his home, he needed to be talked into going to Milwaukee.

Looking to make a signature move that would get his club over the top, Brewers general manager Harry Dalton had a blockbuster trade in the works with the Cardinals at the 1980 winter meetings. Milwaukee would send outfielders Sixto Lezcano and David Green and pitchers Lary Sorensen and Dave LaPoint to St. Louis for right-hander Pete Vuckovich, closer Rollie Fingers and Simmons, a veteran catcher who could swing the bat with authority from both sides of the plate.

But Simmons had "10 and 5" rights, meaning he had spent at least 10 years in the majors, including five or more with his current team. Accordingly, he had to agree to any trade before it could be consummated. He wanted to hear from Dalton and team owner Bud Selig why he should say yes.

"I wanted to know who would be in the trade," recalled Simmons, who also realized the Cardinals were committing to a younger catcher, Darrell Porter. "When they told me what was coming to the Brewers, you could make a determination what the club would look like. If you added Fingers and Vuckovich, the offense there already existed. You realized this was going to be a formidable team. On paper, it looked great."

That forecast proved accurate. The late-season addition in '82 of right-hander Don Sutton was the final piece to the puzzle, but it was the deal for Vuckovich, Fingers and Simmons that made the Brewers the team to beat in the AL East. Not only did it add three quality players — Fingers won the Cy Young Award and AL MVP honors in 1981 and Vuckovich claimed the Cy Young trophy in '82 — it added to a corps of established, savvy veterans who had been around the big-league block a few times.

Simmons certainly did his share to lead the Brewers to their first World Series. At age 33, he played in 137 games, batting .269 with 23 home runs and 97 RBIs. He committed only three errors in 635 total chances, leading all major league catchers with a .995 fielding percentage.

Known to teammates as "Simba" because of his long, flowing mane, Simmons was one of many older players on the club who chafed under the hands-on managerial style of Buck Rodgers. When Rodgers was fired on June 2 and replaced by longtime hitting coach Harvey Kuenn, the players relaxed and began performing to their talent level. As a result, the team took off.

"Harvey was an old-school-er," said Simmons. "He believed in making a lineup and getting out of the way. I'll never forget the first meeting he ever had. He said, 'Guys, there's only two things I'd like to say. No. 1, I hate meetings. No. 2, this one's over.' That's all he said.

"Everybody looked around and said, 'All right, man.' Everybody was more or less freed up to go. We knew how to play the game. You could pitch out on your own, put the hit-and-run on. It wasn't like he was encouraging it. It was just okay to do. These guys were veterans. We weren't going to do anything stupid with the game in jeopardy."

The importance of the veteran presence on the club was impossible to ignore. Though his playing days were over, Sal Bando was still on hand as a "special assistant" to Dalton. Bando and Fingers had three World Series rings from their days in Oakland and knew what it took to win. Simmons and Vuckovich also had mental libraries of vast baseball knowledge and didn't hesitate to share nuggets with their teammates.

"It was really special," said Simmons. "Everybody was helping everybody else. Bando and Fingers had won it all three times. I said, 'Okay, I've been playing a long time, what should I know?' They told me, 'It's just like any other game. Don't make it bigger than it already is. Just play like you're on the playground.'

"It really made me feel good that these guys could help a guy like me, who had played a long time and had some success. It was like a brotherhood."

Those inside the brotherhood learned to keep their guard up at all times. The Brewers clubhouse was a fertile environment for prank-playing, and no one was safe from jokesters such as Mike Caldwell, Jamie Easterly, Gorman Thomas and Vuckovich.

"You were vulnerable every time you stepped in that clubhouse," recalled Simmons. "You didn't know what you were going to get. You would go to your locker and it may not be as you left it. Sometimes, Harvey's (prosthetic) leg would disappear when he was in the shower. Stuff happens."

The looseness and closeness of the club was sorely tested during the season's final weekend in Baltimore, when the Brewers lost the first three games of a four-game series to allow the Orioles to draw even atop the AL East. The Brewers suddenly found themselves in a win-or-go-home situation, in a very hostile environment at Memorial Stadium, the Orioles' raucous ballpark.

"I'll never forget it," said Simmons. "It was so loud, and this is the truth, when I gave the signs to the pitcher, I had to look down at my fingers. I wanted to make sure it was two fingers for a curve. It was so loud I could hardly think. That's what I remember about that last weekend."

Many players on that club suggested there was no sense of panic before that game, no feeling of dread over possibly blowing the division. According to Simmons, however, there was some trepidation.

"Everybody was scared to death," he said. "If we win one game Friday in the doubleheader, we're in. All we had to do is split that. But we lose them both. If we win Saturday, we're in. But we lose that game. Baltimore's fans were going absolutely berserk. The noise didn't stop. That's why I was looking my fingers down.

"After it was all over on Sunday, there was joint relief."

That relief came in the form of a surprisingly easy 10-2 victory, courtesy of two home runs by Robin Yount off Orioles ace Jim Palmer and the clutch pitching of Sutton, the late-season pickup who did what he was acquired to do — win the big game.

Two and a half weeks of excitement followed, as the Brewers rallied from a 0-2 hole to beat California in the ALCS. The scintillating experience of the post-season ultimately ended in heartbreak when the Brewers lost Game 7 of the World Series to St. Louis, Simmons' former club. It was the acquisition of Simmons, Vuckovich and Fingers that paved the way for that October show-down, but by the time the Brewers got there, Vuckovich was pitching with a ravaged shoulder and Fingers was shut down completely with an arm injury.

"You lose your closer and a Cy Young Award pitcher, it doesn't matter what else is going on," said Simmons. "It's tough to come back from that. Everybody was a little banged up, just from surviving the long season.

"It would have been nice if Peter had been sound. It would have been nice if Fingers had been able to pitch. It's just one of those things. Neither one could participate in a way that would have made a difference."

Even more quickly than the Brewers rose to power, they fell into decline. After they faded from the pennant race in the final weeks of the '83 season, injuries, advanced age and trades picked apart the roster. Kuenn was dismissed, and systematically, the players who helped the Brewers get to the game's biggest stage were sent elsewhere.

By the spring of 1986, it was Simmons' turn to say goodbye. In the middle of spring training, he was dealt to the Atlanta Braves for catcher Rick Cerone and two minor-leaguers. Simmons saw it coming and therefore was hardly surprised when the news came to pack his bags.

On May 2, 1982, in Minnesota, Simmons became the first player in club history to hit home runs from both sides of the plate in the same game. Simba, as he was known to his teammates, was well-respected for his baseball knowledge and leadership in the clubhouse.

"It was time to go," he said. "I had served the purpose I was brought there for. I had a right of refusal, which I remember very clearly. I was making a lot of money. They had a deal made with Atlanta and (manager) Chuck Tanner was there. He wanted me to go over there and essentially be a coach. I was a player, but I'd also be a coach because the team was so young and so bad.

"Milwaukee was trying to retool. It wouldn't have served any purpose for me to stay or say pay me the money (in the buyout of his contract) or I'm not going. I saw an opportunity to go to Atlanta and help Chuck, knowing my career was near the end."

Simmons played three seasons for the Braves, during which he began contemplating his future. A thinking man's player if there ever was one, he had forgotten more baseball than many of his contemporaries ever learned, so there had to be a place for him somewhere in the game. It turned out that place was back home in St. Louis.

The Cardinals needed a farm director. Simmons had played with general manager Dal Maxvill, so no introductions were needed.

"I had been in a baseball uniform my entire life and was really looking for an alternative," said Simmons. Being a farm director is a complex job. I said, 'I'll do it. Don't worry about what you pay me.' I loved it. I think it's a prerequisite to being a general manager, particularly today.

"Everyone has this idea that the route to being a GM is through scouting. I don't think scouting is all that difficult to learn. If you're around it enough and see players and have a fairly good mentor, you can learn to be a fairly decent scout.

"As a farm director, you learn not to run one team, but as many teams as you have. When I was there, we had eight. When you're a farm director, your phone rings every day at midnight. You're hoping it's to say, 'We played good tonight.' But that's a pipe dream. You know the reason the phone is ringing is somebody has got a problem.

"It's a juggling act. If you've been a farm director, nothing can shake you at the major league level, if you aspire to be a general manager. Whatever happens (in the majors), you've only got 25 guys, or 40 at the most, to deal with. You call a guy up from Triple-A and the farm director deals with the domino effect."

Sure enough, Simmons' experience as a farm director led to a job as general manager in Pittsburgh. He was lured away by Pirates president Mark Sauer, who previously had worked in St. Louis' front office. It was an exciting venture for Simmons, but that all changed on June 8, 1993. Sitting in his office, he began experiencing sharp pains in his upper left arm. Simmons recognized the symptoms of a heart attack and was rushed to a hospital, where he had an angioplasty to clear blockage in an artery.

While recovering from that heart attack, Simmons began to reassess his life, professionally and personally. Eleven days later, he resigned as Pittsburgh's general manager.

"I decided I had to take care of myself," he said. "Thank God I did. It has been 14 years now and I haven't had another (heart attack). I changed my life and decided I wanted to see my grandchildren some day. I wanted to be around to help my sons. It was the right thing. You either wake up or you don't wake up at all one day. You get sick, and then you get healthy."

But Simmons could stay away from the game for only so long. He had become a good friend of Cleveland GM John Hart, who asked him to join the Indians as a major league scout. Cleveland had become a power in the American League, and it was a fortuitous time to come on board.

"We had six great years in Cleveland," Simmons recalled. "They sold out every single night. Some Hall of Fame names came through there, one after another. That team was built and had so much success. That was a wonderful experience. After six years, the players' salaries got so high, they had to retool."

Simmons decided to retool as well. San Diego general manager Kevin Towers, who had worked with Simmons in Pittsburgh, wanted his minor league system and scouting department revamped. He figured Simmons was the man to do it, and the opportunity was too intriguing to turn down. Simmons spent three years reorganizing those areas of the organization, then settled back into a major league scouting role for the Padres. He was allowed to live in St. Louis, providing the best of both worlds.

"It makes a lot of sense because St. Louis is halfway to anywhere," said Simmons, whose wife remains active in the arts in that city. "It's a nice situation for me."

Defining Moment
On May 2, 1982, in Minnesota, Simmons became the first player in club history to hit home runs from both sides of the plate in the same game.

Number to Remember
Simmons finished with 1,389 career RBIs. Among catchers in the Hall of Fame, only Yogi Berra has more (1,430).

Favorite October Memory
Returning to St. Louis with the Brewers to face his former club in the World Series.

MOOSE HAAS

Physical conditioning always was a top priority for Moose Haas. That's why, at age 51, it looks like he could still pick up a baseball, step on a mound and fire a fastball past a hitter. Only his closely cropped graying hair gives away his status as an "old-timer."

"I try to stay in shape, but it's been a few years," he said with a smile.

Twenty-five years, to be exact, since Haas played a key role in helping the Brewers get to their first and, to this point, only World Series. When that magical season began, the slender right-hander was in a starting rotation that included Pete Vuckovich, Mike Caldwell, Randy Lerch and Bob McClure. A second-round draft pick in 1974, Haas had been a staple in the Brewers' rotation since the 1977 season, posting a career-high 16 victories in 1980 with 14 complete games.

The Brewers weren't a good team when Haas arrived in the majors. In their second season under manager Alex Grammas in '77, the club stumbled to 95 losses. But George Bamberger arrived on the scene the following year, and the Brewers started winning under their feisty new skipper. A heart attack forced Bamberger to step aside after 1980 but the franchise was finally headed in the right direction, advancing to the mini-playoffs under Buck Rodgers in the strike-split '81 season.

Slowly but surely, general manager Harry Dalton put together a veteran-laden team that knew how to win, and Haas liked what he saw happening around him. The '82 team seemed stuck in neutral on the field during the first two months, however, until hitting coach Harvey Kuenn was tabbed to replace Rodgers at the helm. Suddenly, the victories started piling up.

"It wasn't like an overnight light switch that went on," recalled Haas. "What happened is the veteran guys loosened up. Harvey just wrote the names down on the lineup and the guys knew they were going to play when they came to the ball park.

"There were a lot of characters on that team. It was a fun time. Everybody got along. Guys hung out with each other. We all got along like one big, happy family. How can you explain chemistry? You just have it."

Haas, who spent most of his free time hanging out with relievers Jim Slaton and Rollie Fingers and catcher-turned-right fielder Charlie Moore, had an up-and-down first half, splitting 10 decisions and compiling a 4.99 ERA in 17 starts. Looking for the right combination, Dalton, Kuenn and interim pitching coach Pat Dobson later began tinkering with the rotation, and personnel changes were made.

With Randy Lerch shipped to Montreal and both Doc Medich and Don Sutton picked up to bolster the rotation, Haas found himself bouncing back and forth from the bullpen over the final weeks. On September 28 in Boston, he notched his first major league save in a big 7-3 victory over the Red Sox.

"I don't know why they took me out of the rotation," said Haas. "That was Harvey's decision. I wasn't scuffling, but I wasn't dazzling, either."

The pitching scramble continued into the post-season, when Haas returned to a starting role. After losing the first two games of the ALCS in California, the Brewers returned to raucous County Stadium and got back in the series when Sutton pitched them to a 5-3 victory in Game 3. Haas got the ball for Game 4, knowing that another triumph would knot the series and create a winner-take-all Game 5.

"I didn't even think about the pressure," recalled Haas. "You just had to go out and pitch. Back then, I didn't really think about it."

Haas pitched no-hit ball for 5 2/3 innings, allowing the Brewers to take a commanding 6-0 lead in what became a 9-5 victory. The next day, they completed their miracle comeback with a tense 4-3 victory that punched their World Series ticket to St. Louis.

"After we won (Game 4), the pressure shifted to the Angels," said Haas. "We were at home and the atmosphere was unbelievable. It was pretty special to run out on that field at the end. The crowd at County Stadium really energized us. We beat a good team."

Game 4 in the World Series fell to Haas, also. The Cardinals bounced back from a 10-0 whipping in the opener to take the next two games, and the last thing the Brewers wanted was to fall behind three games to one. It didn't look good early as St. Louis jumped out to a 4-0 lead after two innings.

Two runs scored on a bizarre play in the second inning. When Gorman Thomas slipped and fell on rain-slicked grass after catching Tommy Herr's deep drive to center, not only did Willie McGee score from third but Ozzie Smith also raced around from second, becoming the first player in World Series history to score in that manner on a sacrifice fly.

"That was the craziest thing," said Haas. "Gorman went to throw and slipped and fell. Things didn't go well for me that day, but we won. That was the biggest thing."

Indeed, the Brewers did win, scoring six times in the seventh to pull out a 7-5 victory. And when they came back the next day to take Game 5, 6-4, the World Series title was within their grasp. It wasn't meant to be, however, as the Cardinals won the last two games at home to deny the Brewers the ultimate trophy.

"I thought we had a heck of a chance to win (after Game 5)," recalled Haas. "Their speed just killed us, especially at their place with that (artificial) turf. If you walked them, it was like a double. They'd slap the ball on the ground and just beat it out, then they'd steal second. We had the classic baseball team, with power and all that. Those guys were just flat-out fast."

Haas put together another nice season for the Brewers in 1983, going 13-3 with a 3.27 ERA, but he was limited to 25 starts by arm problems that put his career in jeopardy. The season ended in disappointment for all involved as the club fell out of the AL East race down the stretch and Kuenn was fired after the collapse was complete.

"It went downhill after that for the team," said Haas. "A lot of people thought that team would be good for a long time. We had some injuries that really hurt the team. My arm was bothering me. I was never really the same after that."

Haas slipped to 9-11 and 8-8 records over the next two seasons. One by one, players from the '82 team were being shipped away. In the spring of '86, it was Haas' turn to go. He was traded to Oakland for four players at the end of spring training, and his nine-year career with the Brewers was over, just like that. Haas had received advance warning from Dalton, so the move did not come as a shock.

"He asked me if I were traded, what would I like to do," recalled Haas. "I had bought a house in Phoenix in '85, so I asked him to send me to a team that trained there. By the time I got home, my girl friend was holding a sign that said, 'You're going to Oakland.' Harry had called."

Haas spent two injury-plagued seasons with the Athletics, pitching in only 21 games. He tried out with San Francisco in 1988 and gave it another shot with the California Angels the next spring but his arm wasn't up to it.

"My arm hurt and that was that," he said. "At that time I was in to training race horses, which was fine. If I couldn't throw, I couldn't throw. I just went ahead and kept training thoroughbreds. Some got good and we sent them to California, where the money is better. I had a 10-acre horse ranch in north Phoenix."

Haas' love for fitness and conditioning took a unique and somewhat bizzare twist toward the end of his career with the Brewers when he left his wife to live with the club's aerobics instructor. The couple remained together for 12 years, raising horses in both California and Arizona, until they split in the late '90's.

Four years ago, Haas was married to Julie, a native Canadian who skated in the Ice Capades for 14 years. The two met when he was helping to train pairs skaters as a registered strength and conditioning coach.

"Fitness and conditioning has always been important to me," said Haas. "It's a tough certification through the National Strength and Conditioning Association. You have to take an exam, which is pretty extensive. So you really have to know what's going on.

"I'm happy with my life now. I'm with the right person, doing something I love."

Defining Moment

Winning Game 4 of the ALCS against California, evening the series and setting the stage for the Brewers' remarkable comeback.

Number to Remember

Haas struck out 14 Yankees on April 12, 1978, at County Stadium, establishing what was then a club record.

Favorite October Memory

Returning to Milwaukee to a raucous reception from the team's fans after losing Game 7 of the World Series in St. Louis: "The people were great to us."

JIM GANTNER

Twenty-five years later, Jim Gantner still wishes he would have called Joaquin Andujar a "hot dog" a few innings earlier.

It was Game 7 of the '82 World Series, winner-take-all between the Brewers and St. Louis Cardinals at Busch Stadium. Gantner, Milwaukee's scrappy second baseman, was getting increasingly agitated over the antics of the opposing pitcher. After recording outs, especially strikeouts, Andujar liked to point his finger at the hitter as if holding a gun, then bring it to his mouth to blow out the imaginary smoke.

"He was 'shooting' everybody after he got them out," said Gantner. "I knew him from Double-A ball. He was with Three Rivers, with Cincinnati back then. I was with Thetford Mines (in Quebec, Canada). He was a hot dog back then, too, always playing mind games with you."

Andujar was pitching well despite slightly favoring a gimpy leg, the result of taking a shot off the bat of Ted Simmons in Game 3. By the seventh inning, Gantner had enough of the flamboyant right-hander's antics. After Gantner bounced out to Andujar for the third out, the two crossed paths on the way to their respective dugouts.

"You're still a hot dog," Gantner said to Andujar.

The enraged pitcher made a U-turn and started coming toward Gantner, and for a brief instant, the unthinkable seemed possible: a World Series brawl. But cooler heads prevailed and play continued. St. Louis manager Whitey Herzog wisely removed the agitated Andujar from the game and replaced him with closer Bruce Sutter, who finished the Cardinals' 6-3 victory that broke the collective hearts of the Brewers and their fans.

"I always said later if I knew he would have gone nuts like that I would have done it earlier in the game," Gantner said with a laugh.

If anyone was going to be in the middle of possible fisticuffs on the field, it was Gantner, a feisty, gritty, no-holds-barred type who didn't let modest athletic ability prevent him from developing into one of the best-fielding second basemen in the American League. Born in tiny Eden, Wisconsin, Gantner overcame the tremendous odds of playing for little Campbellsport High School and the Division III college program at University of Wisconsin-Oshkosh to become a 12th-round draft pick of the Brewers in 1974.

"Most of the guys had a lot more talent than me," admitted Gantner. "I grew up in a big family and nothing ever came easy. I have to thank my parents for raising me the right way. I carried it over on the field.

"I didn't really think about being an overachiever. That's what people said. I just went out and played hard and said, 'We'll see what happens.' Just being from Wisconsin was different. There weren't a lot of guys drafted from the state."

Growing up in Eden, Gantner was a big fan of the Milwaukee Braves. His heroes were Hank Aaron and Eddie Mathews, so imagine his excitement in 1976 when he made his debut with the Brewers as a teammate of the Home Run King. To this day, Gantner gleefully notes that he pinch-ran for Aaron after he collected his last major league hit with the Brewers near the end of that season.

After a few years in a utility role with the Brewers, Gantner got his big break in 1980. Paul Molitor, the starter at second base, suffered a rib cage injury and went on the disabled list. Gantner took over at second and never relinquished the position. Wanting to keep both players in the lineup, the Brewers later moved Molitor to center before he finally settled in at third base.

Gantner and shortstop Robin Yount soon evolved into the best double-play combo in the majors. From 1981-'83, the Brewers led all clubs in turning double plays. Gantner, Yount and Molitor went on to play 17 years together, the longest stretch that three teammates played together in big-league history. In essence, they became the three-headed Mount Rushmore of the Brewers.

"That was a highlight of my career, playing all that time with two Hall of Famers," said Gantner. "I never could have imagined anything like that. We were close, on and off the field. They were great teammates.

"The Brewers had a lot of lean years in the beginning. I was fortunate enough to come up when we started getting good. Robin had played on some terrible teams."

No player had more nicknames in the Brewers' clubhouse than Gantner. Because of his hard-nosed style of play, some teammates called him "Dog." Gorman Thomas, who thought Gantner moved and talked like the cartoon character "Gumby," dropped that oft-used moniker on him. Reliever Rollie Fingers came up with the nickname "Klinger," after the cross-dressing, lovable character on the hit TV show *M.A.S.H.*

"I got a base hit one night in County Stadium and I was rounding first, trying to take two, when I took a tumble," recalled Gantner. "When I got back to the dugout, Rollie called from the bullpen, right during the game, and said, 'Get Klinger on the phone.' They said, 'Klinger?' He said, 'Yeah, Gantner, get him on the phone.' He said to me, 'Klinger, take those damn high heels off.' Can you imagine doing that right during the game, calling me from the bullpen?"

"Once they give you a name like that, it sticks," added Gantner. "But everybody on that team had a nickname. That's how close we were."

Gantner also kept teammates in stitches with his gift for malapropisms. He had his own way of verbalizing things, sort of a cross between Yogi Berra and Norm Crosby. Asked one spring training what he had done over the winter, Gantner replied, "I went hunting in one of those Canadian proverbs."

Another time, when told that an opposing pitcher could throw with both his left and right arm, Gantner said, "He's amphibious!" Then, there was the pregame workout in which Gantner encouraged a young infielder to "Stay up on

From 1981-1983 Gantner teamed with Robin Yount to lead all MLB clubs in double plays turned.

the palms of your feet."

"You never knew what Gumby would say next," said Thomas, who once turned a pet pig loose in Gantner's dark hotel room to see how he would react. "Half the time, we had no idea what he was talking about."

The prank-playing at times got out of hand, and no possessions were sacred. Once, on getaway day in Oakland, Gantner went to get dressed after the game and noticed his dress shirt was missing.

"I got on the plane wearing just a sport coat with no shirt underneath," he recalled. "I was bare-chested underneath. I eventually got my shirt back. Another time, I got off the plane with no shoes. I took them off on the plane and somebody took them, so I had to walk to the bus bare-footed.

"One time, they cut one of my pants legs off. The pitchers did a lot of that stuff because they had a lot of time during the games. We'd be out there on the field and they'd be in the clubhouse, messing with stuff. You never knew what would happen."

No one looked forward to the daily "flip" game more than Gantner. Hours before game time, the Brewers would gather on the field, off to one side, and play "flip." They'd form a circle and bat a baseball back and forth at each other with their gloves, with tremendous speed and malice in their hearts. If you couldn't keep the ball alive, you were out of the game. Most days, you played at your own peril.

"The flip games were unbelievable," said Gantner. "We'd be on the road and we'd have a crowd behind home plate, cheering for us. Those games got pretty rough. I got a black eye once, a fat lip another time. (General manager) Harry (Dalton) was always worried that somebody would get hurt. (Rollie) Fingers got hurt once but wouldn't say what happened.

"It kept us loose. We were out on the field way early. We'd have a ton of guys out there. Sometimes, we'd almost get in fistfights after the game, in a bar, over calls in the flip game. Even on the road. You'd get the 'red ass' and say, 'How could you make that call?' The next day we'd laugh about it."

Known more for his defense than his production at the plate, Gantner put together a solid season in '82, batting a career-high .295 with four homers and 43 RBIs in 132 games. He missed 30 games with injuries that year but doesn't remember what the ailments were. He does remember how helpless it felt at the end not to have a healthy Fingers to close games.

"We had a lead in five of the seven games in the World Series," he recalled. "If he was healthy, Rollie could pitch two or three innings if you needed it. They had (Bruce) Sutter. That was the difference. When the other team knows you don't have a dominant closer, it gives them a mental boost.

"The highlight of my career was getting to the World Series. The saddest part was losing. We always figured we'd get back again, but it didn't happen. We didn't keep improving. By '84, we were bad again, terrible. I wish we could

Paul Molitor, Robin Yount and Jim Gantner played 17 years together, the longest stretch that three teammates played together in big-league history.

have kept improving. It takes money. I couldn't believe how quickly it all fell apart. A lot of guys got hurt. We needed some more players."

While many of their '82 teammates vanished within a year or two, Gantner, Molitor and Yount played on in Milwaukee. Gantner remained a steady contributor, but the Brewers never made it back to the playoffs. There was an exciting year mixed in here and there, such as the rollercoaster outfit known as "Team Streak" during the 1987 season.

Gantner's last season came in 1992, when the Brewers enjoyed a brief renaissance under new manager Phil Garner, winning 92 games. Gantner played under seven managers during his 17 years in Milwaukee, giving each one everything he had. His toughness in turning double plays resulted in a couple of knee surgeries along the way, but he never gave any quarter, never took any shortcuts. Gantner was the quintessential "gamer," the highest compliment you can pay a player.

When turning the double play, if the runner coming into second was late getting down, Gantner would release the ball low to give him no choice, unless he wanted to take one in the head.

"Teddy Simmons really helped me with that," recalled Gantner. "The one thing he said to me after he came over in '81 was, 'I have one question. Can you turn the double play?' I said yes. He said, 'That's all I wanted to know.' He was real serious. On opening day in Cleveland in '81, Fingers had the bases loaded with one out in the ninth. Ron Hassey hit a grounder to Robin and we turned it. If I had dropped it, Simmons would have killed me."

After retiring, Gantner did some work for the Brewers, mainly instructing young infielders in the farm system. In 1996, former teammate Sal Bando, then the club's general manager, offered him a job as first base coach. But after two years, Gantner quit to spend more time with his four children.

"I said, 'I'll try it and see what happens,'" he recalled. "But my kids were in high school and I was missing all that time with them. I didn't get to see them do anything, so I quit. I loved coaching for Garner. It was great. But I wanted to spend time with my kids."

Gantner continued to do part-time instructing for the Brewers while also finding time to help wife Sue run the River Coffee House, a popular morning café in Hartland, Wisconsin. The Gantners later were divorced, and with his children grown and out on their own, the former second baseman got the itch to get back in the game on a more formal basis.

Now residing in the Twin Lakes area of the state, Gantner accepted an offer in 2007 to manage the Wisconsin Woodchucks in the summer North Woods League, a wood-bat circuit comprised mainly of college players. Where that leads "Gumby" remains to be seen, but his mind and heart are never too far removed from what's going on with the Brewers.

"I might come back to the Brewers one day, you never know," said Gantner, who still dresses out during home stands and hits fungoes to infielders. "I'll always consider myself a Brewer, 100 percent. It's in your blood. It's a privilege to come out here and be around the team. I still enjoy it.

"I really want the Brewers to win again. It's been a long time. I know the fans are waiting for it."

Defining Moment

Batting a career-high .295 in 1982 and helping turn 104 double plays, tops in the American League.

Number to Remember

Gantner batted .326 with runners in scoring position during the '82 season.

Favorite October Memory

Getting to the World Series with the Brewers as a Wisconsin native: "It was something special, being from the home state."

BOB McCLURE

Had he missed the opportunity to play with Ted Simmons and Pete Vuckovich, Bob McClure is not sure he would have become a pitching coach after his long major league career came to an end.

"Ted and Vukie created so much interest because they were so bright about pitching, and about how to go about it," said McClure, now pitching coach for the Kansas City Royals. "I probably wouldn't have pitched as long as I did if I hadn't met them.

"Mike Caldwell had a big part in it, too. They all knew so much about pitching and would talk about it. Simmons had a lot to do with my interest in wanting to coach. He was probably one of the brightest people I ever met, as far as the game goes."

Acquired from Kansas City during spring training in 1977 to complete a deal made the previous December, McClure spent his first three seasons with the Brewers pitching exclusively out of the bullpen. The 5-11 left-hander showed his versatility in 1980 by making five starts and pitching two complete games, while also getting the call 47 times out of the pen and recording 10 saves.

After the Brewers picked up Vuckovich, Simmons and closer Rollie Fingers at the winter meetings that year, McClure eagerly anticipated the '81 season. But he suffered a torn rotator cuff in spring training and was sidelined until mid-September. As a consolation, McClure got his first taste of playoff competition with three relief appearances in the mini-playoffs against the New York Yankees after the strike-torn season.

When the 1982 season began, McClure found himself in a starting rotation that included Vuckovich, Caldwell, Moose Haas and Randy Lerch. Known to teammates simply as "Mac," he took to his new role as a starter, kicking it into gear with a 4-0 record in five starts in June. In fact, the entire team took off that month after hitting coach Harvey Kuenn replaced Buck Rodgers as manager.

"He really let the team kind of run itself," recalled McClure. "We were about to pop as a group. He just let the clubhouse go and let us dictate how it went. We had a lot of enforcers. We had (Don) Money and Vukie and Simmons and Caldwell, guys who had been around a little longer. The coaches didn't have to police anybody. If you messed up, you knew about it.

"I can remember it like it was yesterday. It was get on, get 'em over, get 'em in. The guys really knew how to play the game."

Off the field, pranks were the order of the day in a close-knit clubhouse. McClure often found himself smack in the middle of the action, sometimes on the giving end but quite often on the receiving end. One memorable stunt took place before a Sunday afternoon game at County Stadium. McClure had been out late the previous evening, having a few with the guys, and decided he was a bit too hung over to shag flies during batting practice.

McClure slipped a crossword puzzle in the back of the waistband of his uniform and ducked into the portable toilet in the Brewers' bullpen for some peace and quiet. Problem was, a couple of his teammates saw him do it.

"The little son of a bitch was going to sit in there and work the crossword puzzle while we were out there shagging during BP," said Caldwell. "We knew what he was up to."

Caldwell and a couple of team mates untied one end of the rope on the nearby flagpole and wrapped it around the door handle on the outside of the port-a-potty. The door opened to the inside, so when McClure had finished his business and tried to exit, he couldn't get out. As he tugged and tugged on the door, screaming obscenities, his teammates howled in laughter a few yards away.

"It was like salmon fishing on the lake," said Caldwell. "That's what it looked like. He'd pull the door and you could see the flag pole bobbing, just like a fish on a line. He was sweating like a pig in there. He finally kicked the whole side out of the 'shitter' and got out. The ball club was out there rolling on the ground."

McClure often found himself in both verbal and physical spats with Vuckovich, a constant tormentor. Once, during a heated argument in a hotel lobby on the road, they actually came to blows.

"Here's how it ended," recalled McClure. "I was on top of him for about three seconds, and he flipped me over and grabbed my face and rubbed it on the carpet, and rubbed all the skin off my face. Me and Vukie were like oil and vinegar. He was kind of Teddy's guy. Simmons was trying to teach me and I was real stubborn. So finally Teddy said, 'Vukie, you're going to have to do it.

He's wearing me out.'

"Actually, I love the guy. We talk all the time. We're good friends, very good friends."

As the '82 season progressed, the Brewers' pitching staff slipped into a state of flux. Lerch was sold to the Montreal Expos. In an effort to bolster the rotation, veterans Doc Medich and Don Sutton were acquired in trades. But the major shift occurred when Fingers suffered an elbow injury with a month to go in the season, leading to the decision to shift McClure to bullpen duty in hopes of compensating for that loss.

McClure adjusted to his new assignment nicely, going 2-0 with a 3.00 ERA in eight relief outings. When the Brewers advanced to the ALCS against California, he stayed in the bullpen as Kuenn and interim pitching coach Pat Dobson went with a reconfigured rotation.

"It wasn't that big of a deal," said McClure. "I had pitched in relief before. I never thought about it. A lot of us did it. All you thought about was competing and doing your best to get people out. I didn't think much about starting or relieving. It was just being on the mound and competing."

McClure made just one appearance against the Angels, but it was a critical one. Taking over for Vuckovich with one out in the seventh inning of Game 5 and California leading, 3-2, McClure held the fort with 1 2/3 scoreless innings, getting credit for the pennant-clinching victory when Cecil Cooper delivered a decisive two-run single that sent the fans at County Stadium into delirium.

Rookie Pete Ladd, summoned from the minors to help fill the void created when Fingers went down, handled the ninth and McClure joined the mass of humanity afterward to celebrate a remarkable comeback from being down, two games to none, in the best-of-five format.

"The atmosphere was great during those three games at home," said McClure, who became close friends with 1982 AL MVP Robin Yount during their playing days together. "Nobody had ever come back from 0-2 before. That showed what a great team we had. The guys never quit."

McClure's activity level increased dramatically in the World Series against St. Louis. He pitched five times out of the bullpen, figuring in four decisions with two saves and two losses. The second defeat was the real heartbreaker, coming in Game 7 as the Cardinals rallied for a 6-3 victory to claim the championship. The Brewers took an early 3-1 lead but things quickly unraveled in the bottom of the sixth.

After Ozzie Smith singled with one out and Lonnie Smith doubled him to third, Kuenn summoned McClure to replace the gritty Vuckovich, who was pitching with what was later discovered to be a torn rotator cuff. McClure walked pinch-hitter Gene Tenace to load the bases, then surrendered a two-run single up the middle by Keith Hernandez to tie the game. George Hendrick followed with an RBI hit that delivered what proved to be the decisive run.

McClure induced Darrell Porter to bounce into a force at second before being replaced by Haas.

Afterward, McClure was devastated by his inability to stem the tide with the title on the line.

"It bothered me for awhile," he said. "It was such an important time for all of us. It just didn't work out. We gave it our best shot. They had a good team. We had a good team. But the teams were totally different. They had a lot of speed. We had some speed but mostly a lot of 'bangers.' They had all those switch-hitters and 'jackrabbits,' guys who could run."

Not one to make excuses, McClure refused to blame his Game 7 failure on his workload in the World Series.

"I wasn't tired by any means," he said. "In fact, they talked about me possibly starting in the sixth game (a 13-1 thumping started by an out-of-gas Sutton). They asked me how my arm felt after pitching in four games and I told them it felt great. We had talked about that possibility. We didn't end up doing it."

McClure returned to a starting role in 1983 but missed most of the final month with a back injury, watching in frustration as the Brewers fell from the AL East race. In '84, it was back to splitting time between starting and relieving, followed by a season in which he pitched almost exclusively out of the bullpen.

After spending more than nine seasons in a Milwaukee uniform, McClure was traded to Montreal on June 8, 1986, for the proverbial player to be named later (that player later proved to be the immortal Kent Bachman). By then, most of his teammates from the '82 club were long gone.

"I was a free agent after the '82 season," said McClure. "There were four or five teams that talked to me about going there. I didn't want to leave. No. 1, I felt we had the best chance of winning. No. 2, we had such a good group, and they were all coming back (the next season). That was my favorite time ever. It was a great bunch of guys, a really good team.

"It was a fun year. I just wish we would have won it. I thought we were going to do it the next year, too. We had a heck of a team. Some key guys got hurt. Plus, we were in such a tough division. Those years prior to '82, we won a lot of games. But there was always a team ahead of us, like New York or Baltimore. They called them the Beasts of the East."

Proving the old adage that left-handed pitchers can play as long as they want to, if healthy, the well-traveled McClure lasted into the 1993 season. Along the way, he played for the Expos, Mets, Angels, Cardinals and Marlins. When all was said and done, he logged 19 years in the majors, appearing in 698 games.

McClure spent the years after retirement helping coach son Jake's high school team in Redwood City, California. He also teamed with pal Bud Papadakis to coach a summer league team, winning the state championship twice. After Jake went to college, McClure began contemplating a coaching career in pro ball. He got his opportunity in 1999 when the Colorado Rockies asked him to be the pitching coach of their Class A Salem club. After two seasons there, McClure was bumped up to Class AAA Colorado Springs, where he served a four-year stint.

That path led McClure back to the big leagues. In 2006, he was named Kansas City's pitching coach.

"I feel very fortunate," said McClure, who now lives with wife Shirley in Stuart, Florida. "We're getting better (in Kansas City). It's going to be a good ride. We're building something."

Defining Moment
Moving to the bullpen in the final month of the '82 season to help ease the loss of closer Rollie Fingers to injury.

Number to Remember
McClure saved 10 games for the Brewers in 1980, the season before Fingers was acquired to take over as closer.

Favorite October Memory
Getting credit for the victory in Game 5 of the ALCS against California, pitching 1 2/3 scoreless innings to help the Brewers claim the pennant: "That showed what a great team we had. The guys never quit."

JIM SLATON

The modern-day major league pitcher prefers his role to be specifically defined. Am I a starter or a reliever? And, if I'm a reliever, is it middle relief, late-inning relief or closer?

For Jim Slaton, it was all of the above in 1982, and there was no whining about it. The veteran right-hander had been a starting pitcher for the Brewers for several years but that role changed significantly on a pitching staff influx.

"I was in the bullpen most of that year," recalled Slaton, a 15th-round draft pick of the Seattle Pilots in 1969 who made his debut in Milwaukee two years later. "I was kind of in transition right then, doing both jobs, pitching out of the pen and starting. I thought at that time of my career it would probably benefit both me and the club, to be able to do both.

"I actually enjoyed it. I just pitched whenever they needed me. As far as I was concerned, starting and relieving were kind of the same things. It didn't bother me. It was more common then, not a real common thing, but you kind of did anything you could do to help the club. There was no complaining about it. There's not much complaining when you're winning."

And the Brewers did plenty of winning in '82, thanks in part to Slaton's versatility. The California native appeared in 39 games, making seven starts. He went 10-6 with a 3.29 ERA and recorded six saves, half of which came by covering the final three innings of victories.

Until he blew out his arm with a month to go, future Hall of Famer Rollie Fingers was the closer. But manager Harvey Kuenn was not opposed to sharing the wealth, and did not automatically go to his closer with a slim lead in the ninth as managers feel compelled to do these days.

"There are more defined roles in the bullpen now," said Slaton, well-versed in that area as the bullpen coach for the Seattle Mariners. "Back then, you kind of went with the hot hand, whoever was throwing good, and let him run with it if he was getting guys out. If not, get somebody else in there."

"We had a lot of good arms on that staff. We had a lot of good hitting, too, but Pete Vuckovich won the Cy Young Award and Mike Caldwell had a tremendous year. And there were a lot of characters on that team. It was unbelievable."

Slaton had suffered through the early, losing years of the franchise, when 90-plus losses were a common occurrence. Then, just when the Brewers were turning the corner in 1979, he was traded to Detroit for outfielder Ben Oglivie. Slaton won 17 games for the Tigers that season, topping the club in virtually every pitching category, but Brewers general manager Harry Dalton astutely reacquired him in late November as a free agent.

"When I came up in '71, we were basically an expansion ball club," said Slaton. "We didn't have real good teams in the early to mid-'70's. You could see it starting to change in the late '70's. I was fortunate to be around there to be a part of it. I probably got a lot of managers fired in the meantime. It was nice to be around and see the ball club get into the playoffs and the World Series."

Even with the improved club, nothing came easy. After losing the first three games in Baltimore on the final weekend of the season, the Brewers had to win on the final day behind Don Sutton to make the playoffs. They fell behind in the ALCS, two games to none, against California before staging an unprecedented comeback with three consecutive victories.

"Things were not looking too good against the Angels," Slaton recalled. "Then we came home and after we won the first one, the fans really got into it. I think the fans kind of carried us through, winning those next couple of games. We played very well at home. We felt like we could beat anybody at our ballpark."

Slaton played a significant role in evening that series, notching a save in Game 4. After holding the Angels off the scoreboard for five innings, starter Moose Haas finally ran out of gas. California pulled within 7-5 in the top of the eighth on a one-out grand slam by Don Baylor, and Kuenn summoned Slaton from the bullpen. He recorded the final two outs of that inning, and with Fingers still sidelined, Slaton pitched a perfect ninth to record his first and only post-season save.

Another personal highlight came in the World Series against St. Louis. With the Brewers desperately needing a victory in Game 4 to avoid falling into a three-games-to-one hole, Slaton once again took over for a struggling Haas, this time in the sixth inning with the Cardinals on top, 5-1. He blanked the NL champs on one hit for two innings and was rewarded with a victory when the Brewers rallied for six runs in the bottom of the seventh to pull out a 7-5 nail-biter.

"It seemed like for a couple of years there, I'd come in and we'd be behind or tied, and we'd score a bunch of runs," said Slaton. "The next year, I won 14 games out of the bullpen. I don't think I heard too much about it because the guys said, 'Hey, bring him in. We're going to score a bunch of runs.' With our offense, we were never out of a game. If I came in and we were behind, my job was to hold the score as close as possible and maybe we could score some runs. Most of the time, we did."

When the Brewers' offense came to life again in Game 5 in a 6-4 victory, Slaton figured he'd be wearing a World Series ring sometime soon. But the Brewers went flat upon returning to St. Louis, scoring only four runs in the final two games as the Cardinals came from behind to capture the title.

"We all felt very good, just having to win one game back in St. Louis," Slaton recalled. "They were very tough in St. Louis. They had a lot of speed on that AstroTurf. They could get three or four hits in a row and the ball would never leave the infield. We took care of them pretty good in Milwaukee. We just had a hard time with them in St. Louis. Not being able to bring a championship back to Milwaukee, we were all pretty down after the last game."

Much to the surprise of Slaton and his teammates, the city of Milwaukee planned a parade for the team when it returned home. At first, the idea hit a sour note with the players, still smarting from the devastating turn of events in St. Louis.

"We were emotionally drained," said Slaton. "We said, 'Why would they want to have a parade for us?' We didn't understand the effect we had on the city that year. I went and it's one thing I'll never forget, just seeing the fans' faces. It was just the most unbelievable feeling. We wondered why we affected these fans in that way. You kind of get in your own little world, your baseball world, and you don't realize how you effect other people.

"You're going through the streets and they're shaking your hand and thanking you. You were going, 'Yeah, but we lost.' They didn't care. They welcomed us home like champions."

Slaton enjoyed his brilliant 14-victory season out of the bullpen in 1983, saving five games along the way. But the Brewers faded down the stretch and failed to defend their AL East title, and Dalton began disassembling the team. Five days before Christmas, Slaton was traded to California for Bobby Clark.

"You always expect to keep winning," he said. "You just never know what's going to happen. We had some injuries. That happens. You ride it as long as you can. A few missing ingredients and all of a sudden you're not winning again. As far as being traded, it was probably the best thing for me. I was at the end of my career and I lived in California. I got to play in front of the family. It worked out good for me."

Working primarily in a starting role, Slaton pitched 2 ½ seasons for the Angels before being released. He finished the '86 campaign in Detroit's bullpen, then called it a career. Slaton had pitched 16 seasons in the majors, all but four with the Brewers.

Thanks to that longevity, Slaton still ranks among the franchise leaders in many pitching categories. He is first with 268 games started, 117 victories, 121 losses, 19 shutouts and 2,025 1/3 innings pitched; second with 364 appearances and 69 complete games; and third with 929 strikeouts. He tops other undesirable categories, such as hits allowed (2,054), runs allowed (971), walks (760) and home runs (192).

But that's what happens when you pitch more than anyone else in club history.

"If you ask somebody who has the most wins for the Brewers, they probably would have no idea," said Slaton. "It was mainly because I was there a long time. Twelve years is a long time to be with one club. At times, I was successful. I was fortunate enough to stay away from injuries and pitch a lot of innings. I tried to make it a point to make every start that I could and keep the team in the game. I wasn't a pitcher who could dominate a game, but I could keep it close. If we scored runs, I'd come out on the better end of it.

"That's how I looked at my career — try to stay healthy, pitch a lot of innings and keep my team in the game. I loved my time in Milwaukee. It's a great city, a real good baseball city."

After retiring, Slaton followed the lead of other former Brewers teammates and played a season for the Fort Myers Sun Sox in the short-lived Senior Professional League. It turned out to be a bad idea.

"It didn't go real well," he recalled. "I ended up hurting my shoulder. But everybody was getting hurt. That's why it didn't work. They thought it would be like the senior golf tour. You can play golf when you're old, but you can't run bases and pitch. It lasted one year and then they called it off.

"They played just in Florida. We didn't have a whole lot of time to get ready for it. They kind of put it together real quick and they didn't draw a lot of fans. There are too many things to do in Florida than watch a bunch of old ballplayers pull hamstrings and tear rotator cuffs."

Slaton returned home to Lancaster, California, and opened a restaurant/lounge called Clubhouse 41, a nod to his uniform number. But he missed baseball, and after his two children graduated from high school, Slaton began looking for a way to get back in the game. In 1992, he was offered a job coaching pitchers in Oakland's farm system.

After three years with the Athletics, Slaton accepted a job as pitching coach for the Class A Daytona Cubs. Two years later, he had the opportunity to return home to Lancaster when Seattle offered him a job coaching pitchers at their Class A affiliate there.

"I told the Cubs I was going back home to coach," he said. "They understood. It's not often you get to coach in your home town."

But Slaton didn't stay there long. In 1999, he began a five-year stint as pitching coach at Class AAA Tacoma. After one season as a roving pitching coach in the Mariners' system, he was promoted in 2005 to his current role as bullpen coach. All told, Slaton has been passing on his knowledge to pitchers for 16 years.

Slaton and wife Kelly have relocated to Buckeye, Arizona, a 30-minute drive from Seattle's training camp in Peoria. He often bumps into former teammates, many of whom also relocated over the years to the area. Many remain in baseball in various roles, which Slaton does not find surprising.

"It's probably the love and devotion to the game, or we all need the money," he said, laughing out loud.

Defining Moment

Pitching two scoreless innings of relief in Game 4 of the World Series as the Brewers rallied for a 7-5 victory to draw even at two games apiece: "With our offense, we were never out of a game."

Number to Remember

Slaton won 14 games for the Brewers in 1983 despite pitching exclusively out of the bullpen.

Favorite October Memory

The parade in Milwaukee after the Brewers returned from losing the World Series in Milwaukee: "We didn't understand the effect we had on the city that year."

JERRY AUGUSTINE

It would be easy for Jerry Augustine to look back on the Fall of 1982 with some bitterness. But he decided a long time ago that would serve no purpose.

"What happened was disappointing," said Augustine. "I never looked back. It taught me not to concentrate on the negatives. That will set you back. If you look at the positives, that's something you can build on."

That year, Augustine went from being a valued member of the Brewers' bullpen to MIA once the playoffs began. In a move that still leaves him scratching his head, Augustine and fellow reliever Jamie Easterly were left off the club's post-season roster.

"I was replaced on the roster by Don Sutton, not a bad guy to be replaced by," Augustine said with a rueful smile.

The Brewers' pitching staff was in flux during the final weeks of the '82 season. Doc Medich was acquired from Texas to join the rotation. General Manager Harry Dalton pulled an even bigger trade a few weeks later, picking up Don Sutton from Houston.

In the bullpen, there was a void that couldn't be filled. Closer Rollie Fingers went down with an arm injury with a month left in the season and would never throw another pitch. Moose Haas, Bob McClure and Jim Slaton were shifted back and forth between the rotation and bullpen as manager Harvey Kuenn and interim pitching coach Pat Dobson tried to make the puzzle pieces fit.

"There were a lot of guys moving around," recalled Augustine, a veteran lefty who pitched as a starter during his first three seasons with the Brewers from 1976-'78. "When McClure went to the bullpen, they didn't know exactly what to do because they had three lefties out there. They just said, 'Hey, we're going to move guys around. We're flexible anyway.'"

Augustine made only one relief appearance in September, which proved to be an omen. When official word came that he wouldn't get the chance to experience his first post-season action, it hurt. It hurt a lot.

"At the time I didn't handle it very well," he said. "I really struggled with it. It was a real tough time for me personally. I had some good, long talks with Jamie. Teddy Simmons took me aside and had a really good perspective. He said, 'You know, Augie, if you weren't here, we would not be here.' You learn from those things and you put it in perspective.

"It did take 25 guys, and with us, probably 30 guys."

As with any big-league pitcher worth his weight in rosin, Augustine figures he could have made a difference in the World Series. Not that he could have made up for the loss of Fingers, which many players on that club still believe was the deciding factor in losing to St. Louis in seven games. But Augie would have loved the chance to help in some way.

"Darrell Porter had a World Series second to none," he said, referring to the St. Louis catcher named Series MVP. "I could get him out in my sleep. I don't think he ever got a hit off me when he was in Kansas City. Jamie felt the same way. It was a real eye-opener for me. At the same time, with Rollie hurt, I felt maybe I could have made a difference, made that one pitch. That's the fun about baseball."

Relegated to the sidelines, Augustine decided to make the most of the discouraging situation. He stayed in uniform and sat next to Kuenn on the bench, absorbing the maneuvering and strategy. It was impossible not to get caught up in the tense match-up with the Cardinals.

"I'd go around and talk to guys," he said. "I was trying to figure out the best thing to do. I was a little upset because I was in Milwaukee when that team was not very good. I took the ball every time. Not once did I come down with an arm injury. I did anything they asked of me.

"I really learned a lot about baseball because I sat there next to Harvey. I listened to everything they did. Harvey would turn to me every now and then and say, 'Augie, what do you think here?' He made you feel like you were part of it, no matter what was going on.

"When you looked at it from the outside, it was devastating to lose Rollie. But from the inside, everybody had their chore to do. I think Ted Simmons was such a good leader in that clubhouse. He made everybody feel important in what they did. He would not allow you to not be focused, whether you were the first guy or the 25th guy. That's the story of the '82 team.

"The story would have been phenomenal if we had won it. And we absolutely would have won it if we had Rollie. Not even a question. We might have won it in five games. When he came in, games were over."

Having grown up in Wisconsin, Augustine knew exactly what winning a

World Series would have meant to long-suffering fans there. He was 5 when the Milwaukee Braves upset the New York Yankees in the 1957 World Series, giving the city its only baseball championship.

Augustine was born in Green Bay and grew up in nearby Kewaunee, a tiny village located on the shore of Lake Michigan. He attended the University of Wisconsin-La Crosse, a Division III school, earning three baseball letters. The Brewers took notice and selected him in the 15th round of the 1974 June draft.

"Up until '82, I did everything there was to do," he said. "I started, and then I'd pitch in middle relief. Then one year I was short man. Then one year I was middle man. Then 'just in case' man. I was this guy and that guy. (Pitching coach) Cal McLish came up to me one time and said, 'Augie, I want to come up with a word that describes what you do. I can't come up with any. Do you have one?' We just laughed.

"It didn't make any difference. Whatever they wanted, I'd do. That was fine with me. I just wanted the baseball. It really didn't make any difference. I remember once my wife had me planting trees all day. Jim Slaton had trouble and I came in in the second inning that night and pitched the rest of the game. Was I prepared for it? No. But if you weren't Rollie Fingers, you might be the guy they called on." Looking back now, Augustine figures his desire to stay with the Brewers actually shortened his tenure in the big leagues. He continued in his jack-of-all-trades role in 1983, making 27 relief appearances and starting seven games, finishing with a 3-3 record, two saves and career-worst 5.74 ERA. The following season, after allowing no earned runs in four calls from the bullpen, Augustine was sent to the minors. His role went to Rick Waits, acquired from Cleveland in '83 with Rick Manning in the not-so-popular Gorman Thomas trade.

Augustine sought out Dalton and bluntly told him, "I'll take the ball anywhere and any place and I will promise you I will give you more than he can give you."

"I don't know if they were trying to light a fire under me or what," he added. "I should not have taken the (minor league) reassignment. That's where I made my biggest mistake. If I had declined it and gone somewhere else, I probably could have pitched five or six more years. But I still felt like I could help the Brewers. They were my family. I had been there my whole life."

Despite pitching well at Class AAA Vancouver, including a three-hitter, Augustine was shipped to the Cubs later that season. The next year, he signed with Baltimore and spent the entire season at Class AAA Rochester. Augustine had no desire to return there in 1986, but the Orioles talked him into it. After a couple of months, he decided enough was enough and returned home to Milwaukee.

Two months later, the Yankees called and asked Augustine to report to Class AAA Columbus. If they were in the pennant chase in August, they promised to call him up. Augustine decided to give it a try, but New York fell out of the running and that was that. He would never throw another pitch in the major leagues.

"I don't know if I'd say it was hard going back to the minors," he said. "I was actually throwing the ball better at the end than I did with Milwaukee. I was throwing harder, I had a better breaking ball and I adopted a changeup that I could throw for strikes.

"If I had gone back the next year, I think I could have made it back. But we had twins and I made a family decision. I just missed my family too much. I had five kids and it was time to spend time with them."

Having made a home in Muskego, Wisconsin, Augustine tried to figure out what an ex-ballplayer should do. He studied and got his real estate license. He even took the exam to attend law school but opted against it. He had a teaching degree but couldn't stomach the idea of spending all day cooped up in a classroom. In November 1986, Augustine accepted an offer to represent American Family Insurance, a job he still holds today. But baseball still was in his blood. Augustine accepted a position as pitching coach for the University of Wisconsin-Milwaukee, a fledgling program trying to crack the big-time in Division I. A year later, he was asked to take over as head coach. Well known in the community for his roots with the Brewers, Augustine soon turned UWM into a quality baseball program. In 1999, the Panthers qualified for the NCAA tournament and beat No. 1 Rice before bowing out.

"That was probably the neatest thing we did there," said Augustine. "I'm very proud of what we did there. Every one of those kids was like family. We probably had the worst field in Division I baseball, but we had a lot of heart and we played hard. I drove my own car on trips, never took meal money. I just enjoyed it. It got to be fun."

Augustine became the first coach in school history to record 300 career victories. In his 12 years at the helm, UWM went 347-298-1 and won five league tournaments or regular season championships. After the 2006 season, the three-time Coach of the Year turned the program over to his assistant, Scott Doffek, and went back to concentrating on family life and the insurance business.

"I had been thinking about it for a couple of years," he said. "Division I baseball has really gotten intense. I felt for UW-Milwaukee to take the next step, they needed a head coach that was there all the time. I couldn't do that. I just thought the time was right to move on. My job was done."

Augustine still retains close ties to the Brewers, coming out to Miller Park whenever time allows and taking part in team functions. He understands the ongoing devotion and fondness for the '82 team but also looks forward to the day the franchise will establish a new tradition.

"People really respect the '82 team and I think that's awesome," he said. "But let's move on and let baseball be baseball. Let's not forget the neat thing that happened in 1982, but let's support this team and help make them a winner, too. I know (manager) Ned Yost is committed to doing that.

"I'm probably the biggest Brewer fan out there. I love being around the team. The connection is so close. I've always considered myself a Brewer and always will."

Defining Moment
Augustine moved from a starting role to primarily bullpen duty in 1979.

Number to Remember
In 1982, Augustine pitched in only one game after August.

Favorite October Memory
Sitting next to manager Harvey Kuenn after being excluded from the post-season roster: "He made you feel like you were part of it, no matter what was going on."

CHARLIE MOORE

Charlie Moore could read the handwriting on the wall. More specifically, the handwriting on the lineup card posted on the wall.

Moore, who had served as the Brewers' starting catcher since 1977, knew things were about to change when he heard the news on December 12, 1980. In a blockbuster seven-player deal that would propel the team to new heights, right-hander Pete Vuckovich, closer Rollie Fingers and catcher Ted Simmons were acquired from the St. Louis Cardinals.

"I knew they weren't going to trade for Simmons if he wasn't going to catch," recalled Moore. "I figured I or Buck Martinez was going to be traded. They weren't going to keep three catchers."

Martinez was the one who went, in a trade with Toronto on May 10, 1981. Moore spent that season as Simmons' backup, a role he did not cherish after years of playing regularly. Deciding it was time for a bold move, Moore marched into general manager Harry Dalton's office the next spring and asked to be given the chance to compete for the starting job in right field. That position was in flux at the time, and Moore figured he was the best alternative.

As it turns out, he was right. Not that the transition was an easy one. Center fielder Gorman Thomas, who took Moore under his wing and tried to impart the nuances of outfield play, still laughs when recalling those early practice sessions.

"We'd make him wear a helmet and a catcher's mask to go out and try to catch fly balls," said Thomas. "That's how bad he was. We were in Arizona and it's hard to play the outfield down there, with the sun and all. But Charlie made the transition and turned out to be a fabulous right fielder.

"I always thought Sixto Lezcano was the best right fielder I ever played with. But making the adjustment like Charlie did made it easier for me to play center. Putting Charlie out in right field turned out to be a big thing. Charlie was a great athlete, period."

The main weapon Moore brought to right field was a catcher's throwing arm. It took some time to become accustomed to the longer throws, but the arm strength was there for all to see. And it would play a legendary role in the American League playoffs against California in the fall of that season. Among the league leaders with 13 assists in '82, Moore soon discouraged base runners from trying to take liberties on him.

"I think they saw a former catcher out there in right field and people tried to take advantage of me," said Moore. "They finally found out they couldn't do it. Another thing that helped was playing next to Gorman. He was a tremendous help to me out there. I tried to pick his brain as much as I could. And, being an ex-catcher, I knew the hitters in the league. I probably took more chances than a lot of guys out there because I knew what their strengths and weaknesses were, and how we were going to try to pitch them. I used my head a lot out there. My experience behind the plate helped me.

"When I was catching, I never liked to see balls fall in front of an outfielder. It's hot behind that plate and you don't like to see those balls falling in. I said, 'I'm not going to let that happen to me.' I worked hard at charging the ball. I had fairly good speed for a catcher, and it really paid off."

Never more so than in Game 5 of the ALCS against the Angels at County Stadium. After losing the first two games of that best-of-five series in California, the Brewers came home and drew even with two rousing victories, setting up a winner-take-all showdown with the AL West champs.

Ahead 3-2 in the fifth inning, the Angels were threatening to pad their lead. Reggie Jackson drew a one-out walk from Pete Vuckovich and headed for third base when Fred Lynn grounded a single through the right side. Moore charged the ball and came up throwing, firing a laser beam to third baseman Paul Molitor, who tagged out the stunned Jackson.

A rally had been thwarted, and the Brewers would go on to win the game and the pennant on Cecil Cooper's two-run single in the seventh inning.

"I just charged in and the ball came up perfect for me," recalled Moore. "I just grabbed it and let go of it as quick as I could. I guess it was one of the best throws I made in my career. The next hitter (Don Baylor) got a base hit, also. If I hadn't made that play, it could have been a big inning. That kept the score close and we came back and beat them."

Moore also played a role in the winning rally, reaching on an infield single with one down in the seventh. Proving that sometimes it truly is better to be lucky than good, Moore's well-placed infield blooper eluded diving second baseman Bobby Grich, and the Brewers had a base-runner. Before the inning was done, Cooper delivered the biggest hit in franchise history, a bases-loaded, opposite-field single to left that scored Moore from third and the sliding Jim Gantner from second. An ecstatic Moore jerked Gantner back on his feet in celebration and it was pandemonium in County Stadium.

"Those were exciting times," the native Alabaman said in his soft southern drawl. "Gumby came right in behind me. That's something I'll never forget."

Moore chuckles when recalling a comment he made after the Brewers lost those first two games in California.

"At that time, California had a lot of older players and I think I told somebody, 'We'll get those old guys back to Milwaukee in that cold and wind and we can take them,'" said Moore. "'Get them out of sunny California and back to Milwaukee, where it's 40 degrees with a wind chill of about 30.' The weather at the end of that series was pretty bad. We were used to it, but they weren't."

When Moore reflects back to '82, his first thoughts are not of the post-season, however. He often focuses on the final weekend of the regular season, when the Brewers lost the first three games in Baltimore, setting up an unwanted do-or-die finale with the Orioles on the last day of the season. The Brewers won easily, 10-2, finally winning the AL East after several near misses.

"Baltimore used to kick our butts all the time," he said. "They had those great pitching staffs. So, to beat Baltimore and finally win it, that was something special. Almost more than being excited, I remember being mentally drained after that whole series. It had been a long haul for us, and it all came down to that final day. And then we go out and blow them out. That was something."

Moore swung a hot bat that October, batting .462 in the ALCS and .346 in the World Series. That experience ultimately ended in disappointment when St. Louis won it all in a seven-game thriller, but Moore had reason to feel good about the way he responded personally to the national spotlight.

"I was proud of that," he admits. "I think I had a solid year all the way around, and that just kind of carried over. I tried to step it up a notch. Your concentration level is so high. I was able to perform pretty well. I think we gave away Game 2 (a 5-4 loss in which the Brewers had led, 4-2). We probably should have won that game. You always think you're the better team. It just didn't work out for us."

Moore was known for delivering clutch hits for the Brewers, and apparently had some help in that regard. The Brewers had a clubhouse full of savvy veterans who knew how to get an edge. Simmons, in particular, was adept at stealing the signs of the other club. And, when on second base, he was not above relaying the catcher's signals to his teammate in the batter's box. According to Simmons, Moore was one of the biggest beneficiaries of that subterfuge.

"The thing I remember about Charlie is he wasn't a particularly good hitter until he knew what was coming," said Simmons. "When he knew what was coming, he was one of the best hitters I ever saw as a major league player.

Making the switch from catcher to right field proved to be a key move for the Brewers in '82. Moore was among the league leaders with 13 assists, none bigger than when he threw out the Angels Reggie Jackson at third base in Game 5 of the ALCS at County Stadium.

When we had men on second base, we made it clear to everybody what was coming. When we did and showed the signs, a lot of guys hit well. Others hit poorly. Charlie was the best I ever saw at getting the signs and hitting. He didn't hit a single. He hit a homer."

As it turned out, Moore was not destined to finish his playing career as a right fielder. The aging Simmons began to see more duty as the designated hitter in the next couple of years, and by 1985, Moore was back behind the plate for 102 games. The following spring, Simmons was traded to Atlanta, and Moore split time behind the plate with Rick Cerone, who came back in the deal with the Braves.

"They wanted Dion James to play in the outfield, so I became a catcher again," Moore recalled. "Because of the success I had in right field, it was tough going back behind the plate. I thought I became a good outfielder. I wasn't a very big guy, so squatting behind that plate in the summer took a toll on me. It's hard to stay strong for the whole season."

After the '86 season, Moore became a free agent. He longed to stay in Milwaukee and finish his career there, but the Brewers' offer included a 20% cut in pay, the maximum allowed by major league rules. Moore decided to look around, and initially several suitors showed interest, but the pipeline suddenly went dry. It was a real head-scratcher at the time, but Moore later discovered he was one of the first victims of collusion by owners, a cost-cutting tactic for which they later were found guilty to the tune of $280 million in penalties.

The next June, when teams were eligible to make offers to their free agents who had not signed, Moore opted to go to Toronto. The Blue Jays released him after the season, and Moore decided to call it a career.

"Everybody knows what happened at that time," said Moore. "I had five or six clubs call me, wanting to negotiate. Then the owners had their meeting and I never got another phone call. Nobody would even talk to me. It was pretty evident what was going on. That's why they lost that case.

"That was just a bad time. I don't even like to think of that stuff. I didn't want to leave Milwaukee. I wish I never had done it. Toronto was a good organization, treated the players well. But after all those years in Milwaukee, it wasn't the same. Including the minor leagues, I had been there since I was 17."

After retiring, Moore returned to Milwaukee and did promotional work for a local lawn mower and tractor company. He was offered minor league managerial jobs by the Blue Jays, but the collusion mess left him turned off baseball for a period.

"I just had a bitter taste in my mouth," said Moore, who also turned down offers to work in the Brewers' farm system.

In 1990, a friend back home offered him a job as outside sales representative for Birmingham Fastener and Supply, a maker of bolts and nuts. At the time, Moore wasn't sure he knew the difference between a nut and a bolt, but he decided it was an opportunity he should try. Seventeen years later, he's still with the company.

"I didn't know anything about it at first," said Moore, who has three sons with wife Lynn. "I just tried to do the best I could at it. The last 10 years, I've been their lead salesman. It got to the point where I couldn't afford to get back in baseball. I've got a customer base and it's pretty strong.

"As long as I take care of my customer base and try to add to it if I can, the company is happy with me. I keep making them some money, so they keep me around. We'd probably move back to Milwaukee tomorrow if we got an opportunity. But we're doing pretty good in Alabama."

Versatile as a player, versatile as a businessman. That's Charlie Moore.

Defining Moment

Throwing out California's Reggie Jackson at third base from right field in the fifth inning of Game 5 of the ALCS, helping to prevent the Angels from stretching their one-run lead.

Number to Remember

Moore had 13 assists in his first season as a starter in right field in '82: "I think they saw a former catcher out there in right field and people tried to take advantage of me."

Favorite October Memory

Finally beating long-time nemesis Baltimore on the final day of the season to claim the AL East title: "Baltimore used to kick our butts all the time."

ED ROMERO

When you're backing up an infield with the likes of Robin Yount, Paul Molitor and Jim Gantner, you take your playing time whenever you can get it.

That was the attitude of Ed Romero, who found himself playing in the shadow of a trio of Brewer icons during the glory days of the franchise. Romero made his big-league debut in 1977 but arrived in Milwaukee to stay three years later, just as the Brewers were on the cusp of doing great things.

Signed as a free agent out of Puerto Rico in November 1975, a month before his 18th birthday, Romero played shortstop for the most part during his time in the minor leagues. To stick in the big leagues, however, he had to prove he could fill in adequately at every infield position other than first base.

"It wasn't hard playing those other positions," said Romero, now a minor league infield coordinator for the Florida Marlins. "If you're a good athlete at shortstop, you can play anywhere. My first few years in Milwaukee were pretty tough. I didn't get to play much. The lineup was pretty set. After a couple of years, I started to play a little more. Some of the infielders got hurt."

Gantner missed nearly a month with a shoulder injury in the middle of the '82 season, and Romero filled in admirably. During that period, he batted .309, with a .324 average with men on base, contributing to an offense already firing on all cylinders.

Romero was amazed at how close-knit that team was, playing cards in the clubhouse, going out together after games, pulling all manner of pranks on each other. Then, there were the legendary "flip" games, when 15 to 20 players would take the field hours before games, form a circle and slap a baseball at each other, using only their gloves.

For an infielder, it was a worthwhile session in agility and reflexes. But there also was the danger of personal injury, with no mercy given as the baseball zoomed toward a player's face and other "delicate" places.

"It was mandatory," said Romero. "We'd have nearly the whole team out there playing 'flip.' You had to do it. It was rough at times. I did okay. You don't see players do that anymore. We spent a lot of time together.

"The thing I remember most is what a great nucleus of guys we had on that team. Everybody was great. We were really close. I never played on another team that was so close and pulled for each other like that team did."

Romero played in 52 games for the Brewers that summer. But, as the season progressed and the team moved into the stretch drive in the AL East, manager Harvey Kuenn stuck with his regulars. It still came down to the last day of the season, when the Brewers won in Baltimore to stave off a late collapse and claim their first division title.

Romero was on the Brewers' post-season roster but never got off the bench, either in the ALCS against California or the World Series against St. Louis. It was disappointing to be relegated to spectator status, but Romero understood why Kuenn hesitated to pull his all-star infielders from games. As it was, the Brewers still suffered a heart-wrenching defeat to the Cardinals in seven games in the World Series.

"I think me and (reserve infielder) Rob Picciolo were the only guys who didn't play," recalled Romero, who did get into one game the previous fall during the mini-playoffs against the New York Yankees. "I thought there was a chance to get into Game 6 of the World Series (a 13-1 rout by the Cardinals). I could have gotten an at-bat in that game, but I didn't get the chance. That was all right.

"The atmosphere and intensity were unbelievable in the post-season. There was a lot of anticipation before each game. But, once they play the games, everything goes away. I thought we were going to win the World Series. We had a great chance. Then we lost Game 6. Once you get to Game 7, anything can happen. It was tough."

It took a trade for Romero to finally get his chance to play in the World Series. After the 1985 season, he was dealt to Boston for reliever Mark Clear, who ironically had surrendered a memorable home run to Brewers backup catcher Ned Yost in the final week in '82. The following year, the Red Sox took part in one of the more memorable Fall Classics of all time against the New York Mets.

Romero, who saw action in three games against the Mets, couldn't help feeling a sense of déjà vu that fall. Let's see. We're up, three games to two. We lose the last two games to fall short. Been there, done that.

"It was exactly the same situation as with the Brewers," said Romero. "The Mets came back in the last two games and beat us. Still, there's nothing better as a player and pro athlete than to play in the Super Bowl, the finals of the NBA or the World Series. That's the best there is."

Much to his surprise, Romero found himself back in a Brewers uniform at the end of the 1989 season. He had been released by the Red Sox in August and latched on with the Atlanta Braves. Two weeks later, with the Brewers trying to stay in the AL East race and short of healthy infielders, they swung a deal with Atlanta to reacquire Romero.

The Braves were off that day and preparing for a trip to Chicago. Having played his entire career in the American League, Romero was looking forward to seeing Wrigley Field for the first time. He was packing his car for his family to return to West Palm Beach when notice arrived that there was a message waiting at the front desk of his hotel.

"It was from Bobby Cox, who was general manager of the Braves at the time," recalled Romero. "He told me Milwaukee had some infielders that got hurt, and I was going back to the Brewers. They were fighting Baltimore at the time, but we lost like seven games in a row and that was it. The team had changed from when I was there the first time. I didn't know many of the players."

Romero signed with Detroit in 1990 but was released by the Tigers in July. After playing in part or all of 12 seasons in the major leagues as a utility infielder, his career was done. Deciding he wanted to stay in the game, Romero looked around for opportunities. The San Diego Padres quickly snapped him up, and he spent six years in their farm system, coaching and managing at various levels.

Romero returned to the Brewers one last time in 1997, again serving in different capacities in the minor leagues. He managed clubs in El Paso, Huntsville and Indianapolis, and later served as a roving infield coordinator throughout the system.

"I liked managing a lot, but I didn't think I would stay a manager," he said. "I was an infield coordinator for a couple of years, and I really liked that. It was a lot more fun for me."

During his time in the Brewers' system, Romero had the opportunity to work with some of their top infield prospects, such as Bill Hall, Rickie Weeks and Prince Fielder. He came away duly impressed with those young players, on and off the field, and figured good things were ahead for Milwaukee.

"I really enjoyed working with those guys," he said. "It was awesome. You could see there was a lot of talent coming up. And they're all great guys, too."

Still, there was the tug for Romero to get closer to home in West Palm Beach. When the Florida Marlins contacted the Brewers in 2004 and asked for permission to offer him a position as their minor league infield coordinator, he couldn't say no. Wanting to spend more time with wife Ivonne, Romero figured it was time to take care of his personal life as well.

"The Marlins train in Jupiter, Florida, which is 20 minutes from my house," said Romero, whose son, Eddie Jr., is Latin coordinator for the Boston Red Sox. "I hated leaving the Brewers. I loved the players there and enjoyed working with the other coaches. But I get a chance to go home more often now. That makes it a lot nicer. I get to spend more time with my family."

As for his "other" family, Romero said he'll always remember those glory days with the Brewers.

"It was a great team and a great bunch of guys," he said. "I'll never forget that time. Everybody was so close."

Defining Moment

Playing an entire month at second base in 1982 for injured Jim Gantner and responding with a .309 batting average.

Number to Remember

Romero played 10 games with the Brewers in 1977 at age 19 when injuries decimated their infield.

Favorite October Memory

Getting to experience the World Series atmosphere twice, with the Brewers in 1982 and the Boston Red Sox in 1986: "There's nothing better as a player and pro athlete than to play in the Super Bowl, the finals of the NBA or the World Series."

MARK BROUHARD

When Mark Brouhard arrived in the home clubhouse at County Stadium on Saturday, October 9, 1982, he glanced at the lineup posted on the wall and did a double-take. In the seventh spot was this entry: 7 Brouhard.

He was starting in left field for the Brewers in Game 4 of the American League Championship Series against the California Angels! Brouhard could barely believe his eyes.

Brouhard knew that Ben Oglivie, the regular left fielder, had crashed into the outfield wall the previous day and bruised some ribs. But guys were playing hurt up and down the roster, so Brouhard did not dare dream he'd be playing in Game 4, with the Brewers one loss from elimination.

"We had gotten wiped out the first two games in California, then came back and won Game 3," he recalled. "That made Game 4 huge. If we could win that game, anything could happen."

So, naturally, Brouhard went out and made it happen. Never mind that he would have been the last player in the lineup that day expected to turn in the biggest performance of his life. He hadn't stepped on the field during the first three games of the series, other than to line up for player introductions. With a chance for the Brewers to get to the World Series for the first time, manager Harvey Kuenn wasn't of a mind to make a lot of lineup changes.

"Harvey was an old-time manager," said Brouhard. "He just ran his horses out there every day and let them play. Obviously, it worked."

For one day, anyway, Brouhard joined that team of horses pulling the Brewers toward their World Series showdown with St. Louis. In the second inning, he laced an RBI single off Tommy John that turned into a three-run at-bat when the bungling Angels committed two errors on the play.

Gorman Thomas was thrown out at the plate trying to score from third on Brouhard's grounder to short in the fourth, but the Brewers still scored three runs to go ahead, 6-0. In the sixth, he led off with a double and came around to score on Jim Gantner's one-out single. Capping his coming-out party, Brouhard slugged a two-run homer off Angels reliever Dave Goltz in the eighth.

Brouhard's final tote board: four at-bats, three hits (single, double, homer), three runs batted in, and four runs scored, an ALCS record. Not bad for a guy who didn't think he'd be playing that day. It was a pivotal performance for the Brewers, who completed their remarkable comeback the next day with a 4-3 victory in Game 5.

"I guess you could say my timing was pretty good," he said. "It was one of the highlights of my career.

"It was pretty crazy that day. The place was rocking. You couldn't even hear yourself think. It was a cold, rainy day, but the fans were screaming their heads off."

It was a heady experience for a role player who began his career in the Angels' organization before being plucked away by the Brewers in the Rule 5 draft at the winter meetings in December 1979. Brouhard made his Milwaukee debut the next season, appearing in 45 games. He saw action in 60 games with the Brewers in '81 and 40 more in '82, making the shuttle back and forth between Class AAA Vancouver a time or two.

"I was the fourth or fifth outfielder, depending on what year it was," he recalled. "I was used more for offense. Defense wasn't my specialty. If guys were struggling at the plate, I'd get to play a little. If I hadn't played for a while, they'd send me down to the minor leagues for a couple of weeks to sharpen my bat. They wanted me to stay ready. I remember I had some pretty big hits at the end of the '82 season. I didn't get to play a lot, but I got to contribute to a team that was winning.

"It's hard when you're not playing. Our outfielders never got hurt. I'd go weeks without playing. Now, I watch games on TV and guys are getting hurt all the time. Everybody gets to play. There's a lot more role playing now. The game is more specialized."

Andy Warhol once noted that everybody gets his or her 15 minutes of fame, and Brouhard enjoyed his in Game 4 of the ALCS. He never got off the bench in the seven-game World Series loss to the Cardinals, not for even one at-bat. Even in the rain-delayed 13-1 thumping by St. Louis in Game 6, Kuenn stayed with his regulars.

"That was a little bit of a bummer," he said. "It looked good when we won two of three in Milwaukee. All we had to do was win one more game. Then, we got slaughtered in Game 6. I thought I could have gotten one at-bat in that game, but Harvey was going with his veteran players. He was trying to keep

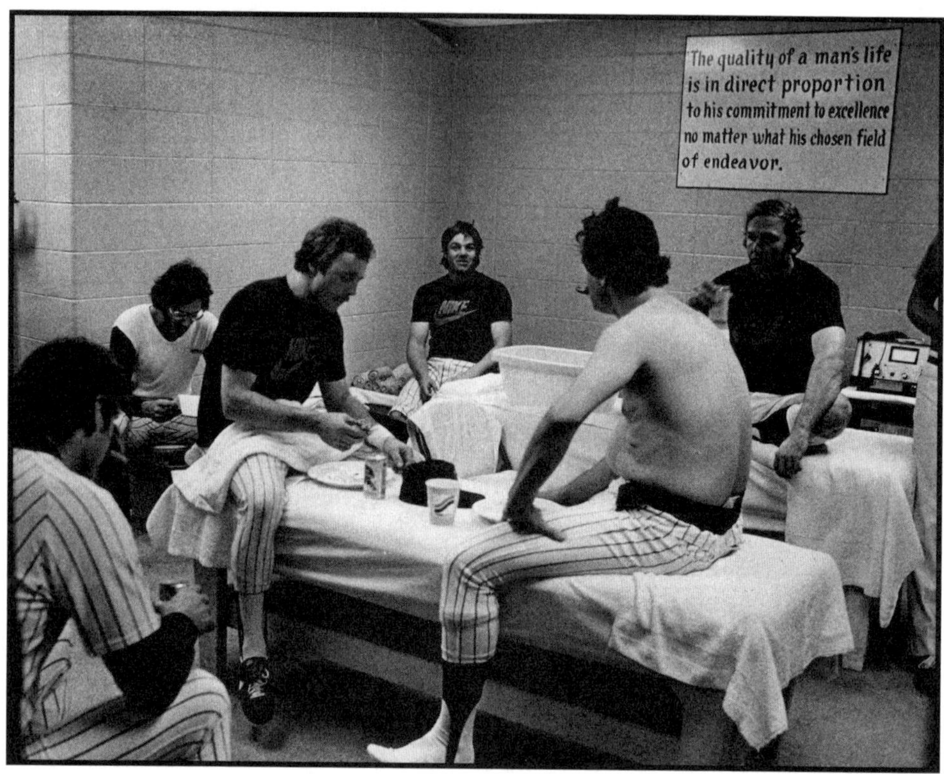

Mark Brouhard discusses that days' game with Rollie Fingers as teammates relax in the clubhouse after another Brewers win. "It was so much fun to be on that team. Everybody got along really well," Brouhard recalls.

the guys sharp for the next day. That was Harvey. That was his style. He went with the veteran players. And we came within one game of winning the World Series, so it worked pretty good."

As far as clubhouse chemistry, it didn't matter how far down the bench you sat. You were one of the guys. You took part in the never-ending pranks, you sat in on the card games and you participated in the daily "flip" games on the field before batting practice. Still fairly new to the organization at the time, Brouhard couldn't believe how lucky he was to land with the Brewers at that particular juncture.

"It was so much fun," he said. "We had a really good team. Everybody got along really well. I had a lot of fun with the guys. We were very close. There was good camaraderie, and that helps make a good team. You had to watch yourself in the clubhouse. They might set your locker on fire. You take it for a while as a young player. Then you start to realize, 'I better give some of it back.'"

One day before a game in Detroit, Brouhard decided to give some back to veteran left-hander Mike Caldwell, who had been on a "hot foot" spree, lighting teammates' shoelaces on fire when they weren't paying attention. Brouhard knew if you sat on the end of the bench at Tiger Stadium, you were directly in the line of Caldwell's fire, literally. So, he intentionally sat there, but he brought along a surprise counter-weapon.

"I went out and sat on the end of the bench with an aerosol can next to me," Brouhard recalled. "When Caldwell came over and sneaked in underneath of me to light my shoelaces, I sprayed the aerosol can at him. I just about blew off his eyebrows. That was the last time he tried that with me.

"I don't know if guys do that kind of stuff anymore. There's too much money involved now. Especially if your team is in contention, you don't want to lose anybody. 'Flip' was great. I don't think anybody ever got really hurt. You'd get some fat lips and bloody noses. They were trying to get rid of it, even back then."

Brouhard accumulated more frequent flyer miles between Vancouver and Milwaukee in 1983, playing 45 games in the minors and 56 with the Brewers. The team remained in contention until the final month of the season, when the wheels started to come off. Injuries and advanced age picked apart the roster, and the club never returned to post-season play.

"It did kind of fall apart after that," said Brouhard. "Some of the guys were getting old. We kind of peaked in the '82 season. When we fell out of it in '83, it took the wind out of our sails. It would have been nice to win it all."

After spending parts of two more seasons with the Brewers, Brouhard figured he'd better try to make some money before his career ended. In November 1985, he agreed to be purchased by the Yakult Swallows of the Japanese Central League. Brouhard, wife Jennifer and 2-year-old daughter Melissa packed up and headed across the globe for a completely new experience and a little spending cash. He played there two years, living in Tokyo and soaking up a new culture.

"I had a good time there," he said. "They took care of us. I hadn't played every day for awhile, so it was a bit of an adjustment. I had to get used to that system. The second year, I was doing pretty good but they brought in Bob Horner. All that collusion stuff was going on in the major leagues, and he decided to come to Japan. I said, 'I could go back to the States.'

Brouhard did so, signing a minor league deal with his original club, the Angels. But he never made it back to the big leagues. After playing a year in the minors, Brouhard decided it was time to retire.

"With collusion, it cost me money to play," he said. "It was time to fold it up. I was offered some coaching jobs, but I saw no money in it."

Brouhard, who had grown up in the Los Angeles area, bought some property just north of there in Camarillo and built a house. His brother was in the construction business, the real estate market was booming and it was time to contemplate a second career. A friend called and said he needed his house painted.

"I had done some painting in college, but I hadn't thought of it as a career," he said. "I kicked around, painting houses, and one thing led to another. I've been doing it for 20 years now."

No longer wielding a brush, Brouhard owns M.B. Painting, a residential and commercial painting outfit in Camarillo. On any given day, he sends out 20 to 25 men to slap on new coats of paint. Once a reserve outfielder at the mercy of a manager's whims, he now calls the shots.

"I really enjoyed it once I didn't have to physically paint anymore," he admitted. He is still married to Jennifer, whom he met when he was 14. Melissa is now 23 and son Justin, 19, is in college.

"I've done well," said Brouhard, who always will be remembered by Brewers fans for that out-of-nowhere performance on a cold, rainy yet glorious October day in Milwaukee.

Defining Moment

Going 3 for 4 with a double, homer, three RBIs and a record four runs scored in Game 4 of the '82 ALCS, helping the Brewers draw even with California: "I guess you could say my timing was pretty good."

Number to Remember

Brouhard's last two hits of the regular season in '82 were home runs.

Favorite October Memory

Hearing the crowd response at County Stadium during his unexpected ALCS Game 4 performance: "It was pretty crazy that day. The place was rocking."

MARSHALL EDWARDS

For a brief, frightening moment, Marshall Edwards lost sight of the baseball.

It was the eighth inning of Game 5 of the 1982 American League Championship Series against California at County Stadium, and the Brewers were clinging to a precious one-run lead. Edwards, who had replaced Gorman Thomas an inning earlier for defensive purposes, now was called on to do exactly that — make a big play in the field.

With one out, Angels designated hitter Don Baylor sent a pitch from reliever Bob McClure on a majestic arc to deep center. Would it be a game-tying home run? Did Edwards have a chance to chase down the ball and keep his team on top? The crowd grew quiet as previously raucous Brewers fans held their collective breath.

Edwards ranged back and looked over his shoulder for the ball. But where was it? The flight of the ball had taken it through the backdrop of the stadium lights as dusk approached. Edwards couldn't locate it, a horrifying situation for any outfielder.

"I knew if I didn't catch that ball, they would escort me out of town," he said. "I said, 'Lord, you've got to help me.'"

An instant from sheer panic, Edwards suddenly heard a voice cry out.

"Look to the right!" said the voice.

Initially, Edwards thought that advice came from the stands. But, upon later reflection, he became a believer in divine intervention.

In any event, he looked to his right, and sure enough, there was the ball. Edwards leaped and caught it before slamming into the wall and tumbling to the ground. A crisis had been averted. The Brewers' 4-3 lead was secure, and one inning later they would be champions of the American League.

"I knew Don Baylor," said Edwards. "I was playing a little deeper than normal. He was trying to make his name, too, trying to produce in that situation. When the ball came off the bat, I knew he had hit it well.

"It was like everything was in slow motion, like you always hear about in moments like that. I said, 'This is a nice dream.' I saw it in the last five feet. There it was. I saw it plain as day. I remember losing my balance after the catch and going down. I tossed the ball to Benjie (Oglivie) and he threw it back in. That was my moment."

And what a moment it was. Of the many heroes that stepped forward to help the Brewers come back from a two-games-to-none deficit against the Angels, Edwards had etched his name firmly on the list.

"I remember that last game, not knowing if we were going to win," he said. "In a short series, anything can happen. You want to see how you will react under pressure. It's something you always want to do. You look back in history at those gallant moments and how people responded. We were able to come through."

It was an exhilarating experience, the kind that reserve outfielders seldom

Marshall Edwards hauls in Don Baylor's blast to the wall in the 8th inning of Game 5 of the 1982 American League Championship Series helping to preserve the Brewers' one-run lead.

enjoy, especially on a team in which the three veteran starters, Thomas, Oglivie and Charlie Moore, rarely sat out games. Called up from Class AAA Vancouver on May 19, Edwards spent most of that season on the bench, waiting for opportunities primarily as a pinch-runner and late-inning defensive replacement.

Along the way, Edwards managed to accumulate 178 at-bats, compiling a .247 batting average. On a power-packed team that seldom put on steals, he swiped 10 bases in 14 attempts.

"I always thought I could play and run a little bit," said Edwards, known to teammates as "The Flea" because of his diminutive size (5-6, 157). "We didn't have many runners on that team. We had a lot of sluggers, some of the best hitters in the league. We had quite an arsenal, up and down the lineup.

"Sometimes I'd play all three outfield positions in a game. It was hard because I had been a starter in the minor leagues. It's something you have to get used to, especially as a rookie. It's tough when you come up and your role changes like that."

Rather than chafe in that ancillary role, Edwards opted to embrace it. He spent eight years in the minor leagues, four with the Baltimore Orioles, before the Brewers plucked him in the Rule 5 draft at the winter meetings in December 1977.

Edwards got his first chance to perform under the big top with the Brewers in 1980. "I was just glad to be in the major leagues," said Edwards, who played college ball at UCLA. "It was a trying time for me just getting to the top. That was an accomplishment for me. That was my role. I had to play that part. I felt blessed just to get the chance in the big leagues."

Edwards' dramatic Game 5 catch was the personal highlight of an ALCS in which he saw action three times, getting one at-bat and scoring two runs. He was not destined to play a role of note in the World Series against St. Louis, however. Edwards was called on just once, entering Game 6 in the eighth inning as a pinch-runner for Thomas in the brutal, rain-delayed 13-1 loss to the Cardinals. The next day, St. Louis triumphed in Game 7, 6-3, and the Brewers' collective dreams were shattered.

"After all we went through, I thought nobody could stop us," recalled Edwards. "When you get that far, you want to go all the way. The greed factor comes in.

"It was nice to get a chance to play in the World Series, even for one game. So many players never get that chance, including some pretty good ones. Just to be there and live the experience was something you always dream about. Everybody wants to play in the World Series. You don't know if you'll get the chance."

Edwards also enjoyed life off the field with his teammates, a close-knit mix of veterans and rising stars. He still smiles when recalling one day during spring training in Arizona when he, Oglivie and Cecil Cooper went to lunch together. Cooper and Oglivie were wearing Los Angeles Lakers T-shirts that afternoon, and thought nothing of it until some of the other customers started whispering.

"People thought we were the Lakers," Edwards said. "They thought Cecil was Kareem Abdul-Jabbar. When we were finished eating, I said, 'Come on, Kareem, let's go.' We just went outside and laughed. That's a year I'll always remember. I look back now and very few teams have that kind of talent. It was a pleasure to be there."

Edwards spent the entire 1983 season with the Brewers, batting .297 in only 51 games. He was removed from the club's roster that winter yet invited back the following spring to Milwaukee's training camp. In the final cut, he was sent back to Vancouver, breaking his heart, and to some extent, his spirit.

"I was kind of shocked when they sent me down," he recalled. "They said my time was up. They decided to go another way. I had a split contract (including lower pay for the minors), so they sent me down. After that, all of the air went out of me. That whole year, I was looking at the transition in my life. I figured my major league time was up. I decided to retire. Cincinnati wanted me and so did a couple of teams in Japan, but I decided that was enough. I was grateful for what God gave me. I had 10 years in professional baseball."

Edwards returned home to Los Angeles and entered the booming field of real estate/construction. He focused for a period on building homes in needy areas of the inner city but later decided it best to relocate to Riverside, California.

"I was doing very well, but then I had problems with the activity of gangs," he said. "Things went better in Riverside."

Edward's wife, Alice, was from Anniston, Alabama, and yearned to return to the South. That sounded good to her husband, who relocated his home building business to that area. Shortly after that venture, the Edwards family moved to Atlanta. Things were going quite well, but one day he heard another voice speak to him.

"The voice said, 'Now, you owe me,'" he recalled. "I remembered that voice. It was the same one that told me to look to the right that day in Milwaukee to catch that ball. So, I was called to the ministry."

Edwards, 54, is heeding that new calling at the World Changes International Church near his home in College Park, Georgia, just outside of Atlanta. Daughter Adrienne teaches math at a middle school in the city and his other two children, Casey and Justin, are enrolled at Jacksonville State University in Alabama.

"This is my new life," he said. "I've been blessed in many ways, including my time with the Brewers. Now it's time to give something back."

Defining Moment

Robbing California's Don Baylor of an extra-base hit in the eighth inning of Game 5 of the '82 ALCS, with the Brewers holding a one-run lead: "I knew if I didn't catch that ball, they would escort me out of town."

Number to Remember

Used as a pinch-runner often in 1982, Edwards stole 10 bases in 14 attempts.

Favorite October Memory

Getting to play in the World Series, even for just one game: "So many players never get that chance, including some pretty good ones."

ROB PICCIOLO

When a player is traded to a new team, especially one brimming with established veterans, he never knows how he will be received.

Rob Picciolo wasn't sure what to expect when he was dealt from Oakland to Milwaukee on May 14, 1982. The Brewers were looking for another backup infielder and Picciolo, a former starting second baseman with the A's, fit the bill.

But how would Picciolo be received by his new teammates? He joined the club in Chicago, and when he plopped down his Oakland equipment bag in the lobby of the Brewers' hotel, some players walked by and shrugged their shoulders in puzzlement.

"They didn't know I had been traded to the Brewers," he recalled. "It was a strange experience."

Picciolo soon learned the Brewers' clubhouse was an entertaining place to be. A bit intimidating as well, but only because the roster was filled with strong personalities.

"I got to know them all," he said. "They made me feel right at home. I felt like I fit right in. I'll never forget that."

Picciolo soon grew close to infielders Paul Molitor and Robin Yount. For a couple of years, his family and Molitor's lived two doors down in the same neighborhood in San Diego. And Picciolo and Yount still get together for a game of golf in Phoenix when their schedules permit.

As far as his role on the club, Picciolo wasn't exactly sure what to expect with the Brewers. He and Ed Romero served as the utility infielders, but it wasn't as if manager Harvey Kuenn was doing a lot of substituting. With Cecil Cooper at first, Jim Gantner at second, Yount at short and Molitor at third, there wasn't a lot of playing time to be had for the boys on the bench.

"I knew going in I wouldn't get a lot of playing time, with that infield," said Picciolo. "They were all horses. They stayed out there every day. I played a few games at second base and shortstop.

"I told Robin that I was there, waiting for him to mess up. He went out and was the American League MVP. I jokingly took credit for that."

Picciolo went long stretches of time without seeing any action. In August, he played in only two games. In all, he got into 22 games, batting .286 in only 21 at-bats.

"I was smart enough to know I wasn't in that caliber of player," he said. "I learned early in my career, if you want to stay around, keep your mouth shut and do what they ask you to do."

Even if they ask you to do nothing.

The lack of playing time didn't mean Picciolo was bored, however. In the Brewers' clubhouse, where pranks were a way of life, you had to watch your back. Nothing was sacred. Picciolo still remembers the day Yount and Gantner stood side-by-side for the National Anthem, both wearing a No. 19 jersey. Someone had slipped Yount's spare jersey in Gantner's locker and he never thought to look before putting it on.

"No one was safe," said Picciolo. "You were on the edge all the time in that clubhouse. It was a fun team. Going on the road was a blast. It was such a talented team. But they knew where the line was, once it was time to play the game.

"We had every kind of personality in that clubhouse. But we all got along. We went out with one goal — to win the game that day. The players were very unselfish. They were a bunch of gamers."

Another lesson imparted to Picciolo was that you better bring your "A" game to the daily "flip" competition. Each day, players gathered on the field hours before the game, forming a circle and batting a baseball at each other with their gloves. Those who couldn't keep the ball alive were out.

"I had to learn real quick," he said. "It was not fun and games. This was serious business. Ned Yost put tongue depressors in the fingers of his glove to make it stiffer. It was competitive. There were some grudges held."

Picciolo developed nothing but respect for the way his teammates played the game on the field. Known for their tough, hard-nosed approach, the Brewers were not a team to trifle with. Kuenn, who had taken over in early June for dismissed manager Buck Rodgers, basically sat back and watched. If a transgression needed to be addressed, on or off the field, the players policed themselves.

"They were able to get on each other in games," said Picciolo. "You had to have thick skin on that team. That was a great attribute of that team. The manager didn't need to say anything. The players did it for him. They accepted nothing less than full effort at all times."

More than anything else, Picciolo remembers how the '82 Brewers never quit. After losing the first three games of the final series in Baltimore, they won on the last day to claim the AL East. After losing the first two games of the best-of-five ALCS against California, they won the last three games to clinch the pennant.

Alas, after going down in the seventh and decisive game in the World Series against St. Louis, the Brewers finally lost a last game.

"That was the key to that team," he said. "We kept coming down to the last game, first in the regular season, then the playoffs, then the World Series. I thought the script was there for us to win it all. But it wasn't meant to be."

Picciolo and Romero were on the post-season rosters but didn't get in any games in the ALCS or World Series. Not one inning of defense. Not one at-bat. As noted, Kuenn was not into emptying his bench.

"I still had fun in the post-season," said Picciolo. "The fans in Milwaukee were wonderful."

Picciolo played sparingly for the Brewers again in 1983, seeing action in only 14 games. Granted free agency, he signed with California. After one season with the Angels, he returned to Oakland, his original team.

Having come full circle, literally, in his playing career, Picciolo looked for a way to stay in the game. Steve Smith, a friend who was managing San Diego's Class AAA affiliate in Beaumont, Texas, helped set up an interview with the organization. Before Picciolo knew it, he was a coach on manager Larry Bowa's staff at Class AAA Las Vegas.

"I liked it immediately and decided I wanted to make a career of it," he said. "One thing led to another."

Thus began a 20-year association with the Padres, the last 14 ½ of which Picciolo spent on the major league coaching staff. Promoted to the Padres' staff in the middle of the 1990 season, he served as San Diego's first base coach before shifting to the role of bench coach for then-manager Bruce Bochy. It was a dream assignment for Picciolo, who had made his home in San Diego in 1983.

"I was very fortunate to coach in the city in which I lived," he said. "I was very blessed. God has been kind to me. It was a lot of fun."

Picciolo was not retained by the Padres after the '05 season and looked around for a new job. Offered the role of roving infield instructor in California's farm system, he immediately said yes.

"I had heard good things about this organization and they were all true," said Picciolo, now in his second year with the Angels. "It's a first-class organization. I rove to all our minor league cities.

"It's very rewarding. I feel I'm making a difference, on and off the field. It's neat to help the young players develop."

During his travels, Picciolo often bumps into former '82 Brewers teammates who are also still in the game in various roles.

"It's amazing so many of the players from that team are still in baseball," he said. "It was a very special group."

Defining Moment
Getting traded to the Brewers, a team headed for the World Series, six weeks into the '82 season: "They made me feel right at home."

Number to Remember
Picciolo started three games for the Brewers in '82 - one at second base and two at shortstop.

Favorite October Memory
Coming from behind against California to win the ALCS: "I thought the script was there for us to win it all."

PETE LADD

When Pete Ladd arrived in the Brewers' clubhouse on July 15, 1982, he was a relatively unknown player, having spent only a half-season in the organization.

But you couldn't miss him.

At 6-3 and 240 pounds, the right-handed relief pitcher was a mountain of a man. And, as so often happens when a newcomer checks in, the established players fought each other to see who could come up with the most appropriate nickname. Or, more often than not, the most inappropriate.

Big Foot. Sasquatch. Largely.

Before long, Ladd had heard them all. And it was fitting that Ladd was a big man, because he eventually would be asked to fill some very big shoes.

"They made me feel pretty much at home," recalled Ladd, who was acquired from Houston after the '81 season in exchange for pitcher Buster Keeton. "I had been up a little bit with the Astros in 1979, so they knew I had some experience."

Those 10 games with Houston three years earlier could hardly prepare Ladd for the role he soon would play with the Brewers. When closer Rollie Fingers was lost for good on Labor Day weekend with a torn muscle in his forearm, the bullpen was put on full alert. Before all was said and done, Ladd would find himself closing some of the most important games in franchise history.

"I didn't really look at it as being pressure," said Ladd, originally signed by Boston as an undrafted player in 1977 out of the University of Mississippi. "Everybody chipped in. Jim Slaton would go in, in long relief, or whenever they needed him. Dwight Bernard, Bob McClure and myself, we would do the short relief."

Over the remainder of the season, Ladd made 16 appearances, recording three saves. His profile was raised considerably in the American League Championship Series against California, when he made three appearances and recorded two saves. The biggest save of Ladd's life came in Game 5, when the Brewers pulled out a 4-3 victory to complete an improbable comeback from a two-games-to-none deficit.

With the tying run on second and two outs in the top of the ninth, all Ladd had to do was retire Rod Carew, a seven-time AL batting champion, career .328 hitter and future first-ballot Hall of Famer. Nothing to it, right?

"I didn't really think about all of that," insisted Ladd. "I looked at him as just another hitter. I knew what I had to do. Thank God, he hit it right to Robin."

That would be Robin Yount, the Brewers' shortstop and league MVP in '82. Yount gobbled up Carew's sharp one-hopper, fired over to first baseman Cecil Cooper and the Brewers had their first pennant. The next thing Ladd knew, a sea of humanity was headed his way, led by catcher Ted Simmons and followed by the rest of the team and seemingly every baseball fan attending the game.

"It was mind-boggling," said Ladd. "Teddy jumped on me and I was able to keep my balance. It was an awesome feeling. But I got a bit out of breath. It was like a claustrophobic experience, with everything closing in. The fans just went crazy."

As important as Ladd was to the Brewers in the ALCS, he became a piece of bullpen furniture in the World Series against St. Louis. He saw action in just one of the seven games, pitching two-thirds of an inning in Game 2, a 5-4 victory by the Cardinals at Busch Stadium. To put it mildly, that appearance did not go as Ladd had hoped.

With the scored tied, 4-4, in the bottom of the eighth with runners on first and second and one out, Ladd was summoned by manager Harvey Kuenn to replace McClure. St. Louis outfielder Lonnie Smith worked the count to 3-2, then took a very close pitch that Smith later admitted could have been called a strike. Ladd and catcher Ted Simmons certainly thought it was strike three. But the only person whose opinion mattered was umpire Bill Haller, who called it ball four.

By his own admission, Ladd became unraveled by that call.

"I should have gotten over it, but the 'youngness' in me came out and I didn't," he recalled. "I thought the umpire was calling it really tight but that happens."

Unable to regain his composure, Ladd walked pinch-hitter Steve Braun on four pitches, none close to the strike zone. The bases-loaded walk allowed George Hendrick to trot home with what proved to be the winning run.

Of course, it never would have come down to that had the Brewers been able to hang on to a 3-0 lead built in their first three at-bats. But pitcher Don

Pete Ladd recorded the biggest save of his life when he got seven-time AL batting champion, Rod Carew, to hit a one-hopper right at Brewers shortstop Robin Yount who fired over to first baseman Cecil Cooper to clinch Game 5 of the ALCS and give the Brewers the American League pennant.

Sutton, who won do-or-die games on the final day of the regular season in Baltimore as well as Game 5 of the ALCS, was running on fumes, and St. Louis finally pulled even on Darrell Porter's two-run, opposite-field double in the sixth inning.

Still, Ladd felt responsible for the defeat. Whether Kuenn lost faith in him or not after that outing, only Kuenn knew. But Ladd never threw another pitch in the World Series. He preferred to believe it had more to do with match-ups.

"Being a left-hander, and having so many left-handed bats in the St. Louis lineup, Bob McClure was used more often," said Ladd. "He was the man to go in, and understandably so. I wanted to pitch a lot but it didn't happen. Still, I wouldn't trade it for anything, to go through that experience. Harvey did what he thought was right, and I backed him up all the way."

Ladd's teammates backed the big reliever as well. They knew Milwaukee wouldn't have been playing in the World Series if not for the job he did over the final weeks of the season, not to mention the ALCS.

"We did miss Rollie, but Peter Ladd did a phenomenal job," said right fielder Charlie Moore. "I think he got squeezed in that one game in the World Series.

He did a great job. I couldn't say enough about the way he stepped in and did what he did. You would have thought he was a veteran of many years, the way he pitched."

Even with that Game 2 disappointment, the Brewers took two of three at home to go ahead in the World Series. Needing one more victory to claim the title, they lost the last two games in St. Louis.

"Oh, gosh yes, I thought we'd win," said Ladd. "We all did. We were going to St. Louis, one of the toughest parks to play in, but we just had to win one game. Game 7 was a great game. Unfortunately, we came up short. In the eighth and ninth innings, I was up in the pen. For me to come in, it probably would have had to be a tied game. We fought hard."

With Fingers out the entire '83 season, Ladd again found himself closing games for the Brewers, notwithstanding a one-month assignment with Class AAA Vancouver. In 44 appearances, he recorded 25 saves, compiling a sparkling 2.55 ERA in the process. Despite Ladd's nine saves in the final month, the Brewers faded from the pennant race, finishing in fifth place, 11 games out.

Fingers returned in 1984, and though far from the dominant reliever of previous years, he resumed his role as the closer. Ladd slid into a set-up role, but the team slid much farther. Remarkably, the Brewers were bad again that year, losing 94 times. There was little improvement in 1985, and Ladd was released that winter. The team's roster was turning over, and Big Foot joined the casualty list.

"By '83, we had done most of the damage we could do," he said. "When it didn't happen, it was time to change. It was hurtful when they released me, but I understood. It was a business decision."

Ladd signed with Seattle and did a fine job for the Mariners in 1986, going 8-6 with a 3.82 ERA and six saves in 52 appearances. One of his teammates was Gorman Thomas, the former fan favorite in Milwaukee who was traded to Cleveland in the middle of the '83 season. Ladd injured his shoulder late in that campaign and was released the following spring by the Mariners. He signed with the Los Angeles Dodgers and spent the entire year at Class AAA Albuquerque before deciding it was time to retire.

The Ladd family moved to Tucson, the hometown of wife Eve. They had a daughter, Lindsey, and settled in for the long haul. Ladd took a job as a service writer in the automotive business, a position he held for 10 years before deciding "I didn't like it anymore." He went to work as a driver — and later, route manager — for Schwan's, a frozen food delivery service.

"It was a lot of fun," he said. "I put in 15-hour days, about four or five days a week, so it took away a lot of my family time. I went into some 'unwanted' parts of Arizona, but it worked out okay."

Ladd certainly wasn't averse to trying unusual jobs. During his playing days with the Brewers, he spent his off-seasons as a probation and parole officer at the Cumberland County Jail in Portland, Maine, his hometown. He had been a criminal justice major in college and figured he would apply that field of study when not throwing a baseball.

"I had this non-paying internship, but I wanted to make some money so I went to the sheriff and he hired me to work at the jail," recalled Ladd. "I did it for five off-seasons."

Three years ago, Ladd convinced his wife to abandon the desert and move to Portland, where the only cactus you'll see is in a nursery hothouse. Ready for yet another new work experience, he took a job with a local lumber company, in contract sales. The way he saw it, job security would not be a problem.

"We have a lot of trees in Maine," he said.

Ladd still keeps in touch with many of his former Brewer teammates. He has made appearances in Milwaukee's fantasy camp in Phoenix, always eager to talk about the '82 season, when Sasquatch became more than a rural legend.

"We see each other and it's like no time has passed at all," he said. "There are so many stories. It's unbelievable. The guys on that team were really close. On the road, you could take a team picture in the bar every night."

Defining Moment

Saving the decisive Game 5 of the ALCS against the California Angels: "It was an awesome feeling."

Number to Remember

Ladd pitched a total of 3 1/3 innings in the ALCS, allowing no hits and no walks, and striking out five.

Favorite October Memory

Being on the mound when the Brewers clinched their first pennant: "It was mind-boggling. The fans just went crazy."

GEORGE "DOC" MEDICH

Doc Medich might have been the first to realize just how badly Rollie Fingers was injured.

Medich, who went by "Doc" rather than his given name George because he was interning to be an orthopedist, happened to be in the trainer's room in the Brewers' clubhouse at County Stadium on September 2, 1982, when Fingers walked in. The reigning Cy Young Award winner and AL MVP had been removed from the first game of a doubleheader against Cleveland in the ninth inning after feeling something tear in his upper forearm.

"I think I did something to my elbow," Fingers told trainers John Adam and Freddie Frederico.

Medich took a look at Fingers' arm and couldn't hold back his startled reaction.

"Oh, oh," he said. "This isn't good."

"I could see this wad of muscle had separated from the bone," recalled Medich, who was doing his internship at the University of Pittsburgh Medical Center during his off-seasons. "I knew right away he had ruptured the flexor muscle and torn the tendon off. I knew exactly what would happen next, what it would take to fix it. I knew he wouldn't be back that season. There was no doubt what it was. I was probably the first to 'diagnose' it."

Unfortunately for the Brewers and Fingers, Medich's medical training had made him an accurate judge of the severity of the injury. Fingers wouldn't pitch again that season, and though the Brewers would go on to win the AL East as well as the ALCS against California, the mustachioed closer was badly missed in the seven-game loss to the St. Louis Cardinals in the World Series.

It was the acquisition of Medich in mid-August, and veteran Don Sutton a couple of weeks later, which allowed the Brewers to move starters Bob McClure and Moose Haas into the bullpen over the final month to help ease the loss of Fingers. Medich was playing for the Texas Rangers, who were in the midst of a 98-loss season, when he approached owner Eddie Chiles with a request.

"If you're not going to bring me back next year, all I'm doing is taking up space," Medich told Chiles. "I'd like to go to a pennant contender if you could do it."

Medich didn't tell Chiles he already had planned to retire after the '82 season. The gracious owner honored his request and sold him to the Brewers on August 11. Three days later, the Brewers sent lefty Randy Lerch to Montreal to clear a spot in the starting rotation. Not long after arriving in the Milwaukee clubhouse, Medich realized he had hit the baseball jackpot.

"It was a lot different," he said. "Right away, we were playing for something important. In Texas, we weren't going to win anything. We played hard, but we weren't going anywhere. The Brewers had more at stake. The games meant more."

Medich didn't have to be introduced to interim pitching coach Pat Dobson, who was filling in for ailing Cal McLish. Medich and Dobson had been teammates on the New York Yankees' pitching staff in the mid-70s. Medich only wished he had more gas remaining in his pitching tank when he joined the Brewers.

"I had contracted hepatitis in spring training that year," he recalled. "I could go six innings really good, then I'd get tired. My pitches started slowing down. I fought that all year. I never wanted to come out of a ballgame, but I'd get tired."

In 10 starts with the Brewers, Medich battled to a 5-4 record and 5.00 ERA. He remained on the active roster for the post-season but was not surprised when manager Harvey Kuenn opted not to pitch him during the club's dramatic comeback against the Angels in the five-game ALCS.

"I wasn't pitching very well at the end of the season," said Medich. "I was hanging by a thread, really. I probably needed a month off at that point. Harvey used guys that were pitching well, and I couldn't blame him."

Medich played the role of spectator in the World Series as well until getting an unexpected opportunity in the dreadful 13-1 loss to the Cardinals in Game 6. Play was halted for more than two hours by rain in the sixth inning, with St. Louis cruising, 8-0, behind John Stupor. No World Series game had been shortened by rain and Commissioner Bowie Kuhn wasn't going to let it happen on his watch, so play finally was resumed after the long delay.

With the game out of hand, Dobson approached Medich and asked if he wanted to get in the game. Days away from announcing his retirement, Medich figured it would be nice to say he once pitched in the World Series. It wasn't pretty, as Medich struggled with the elements as well as rustiness after many days of inactivity, surrendering five hits and six runs in two innings.

"I pitched just to say I pitched in the World Series," he said. "It was really wet out there. I threw one pitch three feet behind the hitter. I remember telling the umpire, 'It's too slippery to pitch.'

"St. Louis had a really good team. So did we. There were contrasting styles. That's what the World Series is all about."

During his down time earlier in the Series, Medich approached the Cardinals' Bruce Sutter in the outfield during batting practice. Always possessing an inquisitive mind, Medich wanted to hear about the pitch Sutter was using to torment hitters and evolve as one of the top closers in the game.

"He said it was a split-finger fastball," recalled Medich. "It was a terminology that was new to the game. What he did differently was put the ball at the end of his fingers. He had the same arm motion (as a fastball) but the ball didn't go as fast, and it went down. He was really the first to use that pitch to that extent and with that much success. Now, everybody is throwing it."

After the season, Medich figured it was time to devote all of his energy to his next career as an orthopedic specialist. He returned home to Aliquippa, Pennsylvania, and spent five months in a physical medicine residency at Pitt. After that came a full-time orthopedic residency.

"I was at Pitt for a long time," said Medich. "I went to school there for the first time in 1966 and finished my residency there in '86, so I was there 20 years."

Because of his background as a pitcher, Medich had become keenly interested in sports medicine. He decided to accept a residency with Dr. James Andrews, who was building what would become one of the premier sports medicine clinics in the country in Birmingham, Alabama. Andrews was a pioneer in arthroscopic surgery, a less-invasive procedure than open surgery that allowed athletes to return to competition much sooner. Medich quickly became fascinated with that field.

"He was pushing the envelope," said Medich. "Shoulder arthroscopy was new back then. That's what he did. I was there to learn. I got in there and did some of the procedures. Most of the stuff we did was arthroscopic."

On occasion, Medich would see familiar faces come to the clinic for treatment of injuries. Baseball players were starting to flock to Birmingham, hearing the success stories of previous patients.

"They'd come in and say, 'I know you,'" said Medich. "I'd say, 'I used to be 60 feet, 6 inches in front of you.'"

After a year working with Andrews, Medich returned to Aliquippa and joined a private practice as a general orthopedist. For the next 15 years, he treated patients before retiring at the turn of the century. Along the way, however, he fell into the trap of many doctors, becoming a self-medicator.

With lots of residual aches and pains from years of trying to throw baseballs past hitters, Medich regularly took painkillers. In an all-too-common story, he became addicted to them. And, as so often happens, Medich got caught. In 2001, he pleaded guilty to 12 counts of writing false prescriptions for painkillers that he filled for his own use. Medich was placed on nine years probation and ordered to enter a rehabilitation program.

"Addiction has been a part of my life," he said. "I don't mind talking about it. I'm not embarrassed by it. Obviously, I wish it didn't happen. I've been clean since '99, since I got away from medicine. I don't think that's a coincidence. When you're a doctor, you get up in the morning and ask yourself, 'How am I going to keep from being sued today?' That's what it has come to. Doctors still tell me that. It's not a comfortable way to live."

Medich enjoys spending time with wife Donna and their two children, Kelly, a teacher in Pittsburgh, and Nicky, who works for a mortgage company. For those who think retirement overloads a person with idle time, Medich begs to differ.

"I'm so busy, but I can't tell you what I do," he joked. "I got interested in the basic sciences again, particularly the physics of golf. I wanted to find out about flex and torque and all of that. The next thing I knew, I had all this club-making equipment in my basement. I don't do it full-time and I don't advertise it.

"I also started studying astronomy. It's something I really like. I'm not just looking through the telescope, up in the sky. It's more than that. Actually, we're in the golden age of astronomy. They're discovering something new every day. They're finding some interesting things."

As for the decision to declassify Pluto as a planet, Medich laughed and said, "I don't think Pluto is out there worrying about its status."

Defining Moment

Being traded from the downtrodden Texas Rangers to the playoff-bound Brewers in mid-August: "The Brewers had more at stake. The games meant more."

Number to Remember

Medich made 10 starts for the Brewers in '82, going 5-4 with a 5.00 ERA.

Favorite October Memory

Getting to pitch in the World Series, even if it was the lopsided Game 6 defeat: "I pitched just to say I pitched in the World Series."

RANDY LERCH

The way Randy Lerch saw it, few things could replicate the adrenaline rush of standing on a mound in the major leagues, facing the other team's best hitter with the bases loaded.

Operating a backhoe was one of those few things.

"I always liked heavy equipment," said Lerch, who taught that job specialty for Irish Construction in Penn Valley, California, for the past dozen or so years. "It's the closest thing I could ever get as far as digging around stuff that could blow you up. It's just like being on the mound in the big leagues."

A left-handed pitcher selected in the eighth round of the 1973 draft out of California's Cordova High School by Philadelphia, Lerch made his major-league debut two years later at the tender age of 20. By 1977, he was in the Phillies' starting rotation, a position he held until the spring of 1981, when two weeks into training camp in Clearwater, Florida, he was traded to the Brewers for reserve outfielder Dick Davis.

Lerch knew very little about his new club. He did remember seeing shortstop Robin Yount in his only season in the minors in 1973 at Class A Newark of the New York-Penn League. Lerch was pitching for Auburn and used to watch the wiry 17-year-old Yount take infield on the rough surface of his home ballpark.

"That field in Newark was so bad," recalled Lerch. "It was like having boulders in the infield. They used to come out early every day and hit grounders to Robin as hard as they could. He was incredible, out there battling those bad hops."

When Lerch reported to the Brewers' training camp in Sun City, Arizona, he discovered something else about his new club: there was a tremendous amount of talent in that clubhouse.

"I didn't realize until I got there how good that team was," he said. "Then I got there and said, 'Holy cow.' It was way weird. I had never been traded before. I didn't know what to do with myself. Luckily, Gorman Thomas took me around and introduced me to everybody. That really helped.

"Sal Bando was there, who I looked up to, and Rollie Fingers. Sal was always calling Rollie "buzzard." Pete Vuckovich and Ted Simmons had come over from St. Louis, too. We had a lot of people from a lot of organizations with great talent. I had come up with a lot of winning teams in Philly. They weren't getting a 'cherry.' I had been on division champions."

Lerch began the year in the bullpen but soon moved into the starting rotation. A player strike cut that season in half, and when play resumed from scratch in the second half, Lerch was on top of his game. He pitched the Brewers to big victories over AL East rivals Baltimore, New York and Boston during the stretch run, helping his new team claim the second-half title and its first playoff berth in the division series against the Yankees.

"I felt like I was home again," said Lerch. "I didn't have a great career as far as wins and losses (60-64) and stats, but a lot of great players like Ernie Banks never won anything. To be on teams that won all the time was incredible."

After the Brewers lost the first two games to New York at County Stadium, Lerch was given the ball in Game 3 at Yankee Stadium. It was a win-or-go-home situation in the best-of-five format, playing in the most intimidating road venue in the league, with 56,411 screaming fans in the stands. No big deal. Not much pressure.

Pitching on his 27th birthday, Lerch responded by limiting the mighty Yankees to three hits and one run over six innings. He exited with a 3-1 lead, but Fingers surrendered two runs in the bottom of the seventh in a nail-biter the Brewers later pulled out, 5-3, to stay alive. Milwaukee would win the next day, also, to even the series before losing in the decisive Game 5.

"I remember to this day (general manager) Harry Dalton and (team president) Bud Selig saying what a great job I did," Lerch recalled. "That meant a lot to me."

Lerch's second season with the Brewers got off to an ignominious start. Heavy rain showers forced the cancellation of practice one day during spring training at Sun City Stadium, but a group of pitchers whose day it was to throw hung around to get their work in. Boys will be boys, and one thing led to another, and the next thing you knew, a mud-ball battle had begun on the rain-soaked field.

Fingers tried to sneak up behind Lerch and dump mud on his head, but Lerch saw him coming, wheeled around and tossed the reigning Cy Young Award winner and AL MVP to the ground. Fingers landed hard on his left shoulder.

"Oh, my shoulder," moaned Fingers.

"Stop screwing around," replied Lerch, who thought the future Hall of Famer was teasing.

Suddenly, Lerch realized the gravity of the situation. Fingers had suffered a slight separation of the shoulder. Luckily for all involved, it was his non-throwing shoulder. But both pitchers understood there would be hell to pay in any event. So, they made up a story. They said Fingers was hurt during a "flip" game, the daily competition in which players gathered in a circle and batted a baseball at each other with vigor.

"After that, they wouldn't let us play 'flip' until finally, we told them what really happened," said Lerch. "I was later told by a couple of investors in the team if I even looked at Rollie strange again, I'd be gone. We were just having fun, but this was the Cy Young winner and MVP we're talking about."

Things went only slightly better for Lerch once the regular season began. He fell into a win-one, lose-one mode, unable to get on a roll and string together victories. The other members of the rotation, Pete Vuckovich, Mike Caldwell, Moose Haas and Bob McClure, were putting together nice seasons, but Lerch struggled to stay at .500.

"I was inconsistent, like I was my whole career," he said. "There were games I should have won that I didn't. It was both good and bad."

When the Brewers purchased veteran right-hander Doc Medich from Texas on August 11, Lerch figured his days were numbered. As it turned out, it was a low number. Three days later, he was sold to the Montreal Expos. At the time, Lerch was 8-7 with a 4.97 ERA in 20 starts.

"I was struggling at the time, so it didn't surprise me," said Lerch. "At the same time, I didn't really expect it. I had gotten close to Jim Slaton and it hurt having to say goodbye. Going to Montreal was like being in a whole different world. The crowds weren't very good. It was different. It was always a pain in the ass to go through customs to go there when I played in Philly.

"I still followed the Brewers. I considered a lot of those guys my friends."

Watching from afar, Lerch saw the Brewers win on the last day of the season in Baltimore to win their division, rally from a two-games-to-none hole in the ALCS to beat California, and advance to the World Series, where they lost in hearthreaking fashion to St. Louis in seven games. Lerch couldn't help thinking back to his 1980 season with Philadelphia, when he was left off the World Series roster as the Phillies toppled Kansas City for the title.

"I felt like I was cheated," he said. "It hurt a lot. I could have enjoyed it. I was upset. I would have loved to have been there. It breaks your heart. You realize it's a business, but it still hurts."

Lerch was released by Montreal in the middle of the '83 season and latched on with San Francisco. Two years later, he signed with his original team, pitching for Philadelphia for one year before retiring.

"It was pretty cool to go back to Philly," he said. "I was a baby in the big leagues with them at age 20. It was like going back to the womb."

After retiring, Lerch searched for a new career. He went into the restaurant business for a short spell, but that didn't work out. Lerch finally reached out to his best friend in the game, former Phillies closer Tug McGraw.

"We were very close," he said. "We called ourselves the 'Dynamic Duo.' I was down on my luck and called Tug for advice. He was doing his 'You Gotta Believe' radio show, something really positive, and he said, 'Come back to Philly.' I did, and he introduced me to some people, and I went and played in the Senior Professional Baseball League in Florida. There were a lot of great old names there. But it was a very different game."

When that circuit folded, McGraw hooked Lerch up with some friends in the construction business in New Jersey. That venture didn't last long, and Lerch decided to return to California. Soon afterward, he latched on with Irish Construction, and has been there ever since. He's now an area manager in charge of 80 employees but still enjoys passing on the skills of operating heavy equipment.

"You have your balls in your hands," he said. "It's very powerful and scary at the same time. I absolutely love it. When you're babied from the time you're out of high school and get into professional sports, it's all you ever know. But I had worked in the fields and orchards as a kid, riding a tractor."

Lerch, who had two children, Kristy and Randy Jr., with wife Janet before getting divorced, plans to marry his fiancée, Maria, later this year. Now a grandfather and living in Gilroy, California, not far from San Jose, he regrets not staying in closer contact with his former Brewers teammates.

"I apologize to all of them," he said. "I really don't stay in touch. I love those guys, but I've tried to focus more on the future. I'm sorry, but that's the way I look at it. It was a great experience, but I needed to turn the page on my life. I appreciate my new life."

Defining Moment

Getting traded to the Brewers during spring training in 1981 for reserve outfielder Dick Davis: "I didn't realize until I got there how good that team was."

Number to Remember

Lerch made 20 starts for the Brewers in '82 before being sold to Montreal in mid-August: "I was inconsistent, like I was my whole career."

Favorite October Memory

Pitching six strong innings to help the Brewers win Game 3 of the 1981 Divisional Series against New York at Yankee Stadium.

ROY HOWELL

By the time Roy Howell signed with the Brewers as a free agent on December 23, 1980, he had experienced enough losing. The veteran third baseman played the previous four seasons with the Toronto Blue Jays, the first four years of the franchise's existence.

They were four truly ugly years. The Blue Jays lost 107 games on their maiden voyage in 1977, followed by seasons of 102 losses, 109 losses and a mere 95 losses in 1980.

There was little wonder that Howell gave himself an early Christmas present by signing with the Brewers, who had turned the corner after years of losing and were an emerging force in the rugged AL East.

"I was getting to play every day, but we were losing a hundred games every year," said Howell, who began his career with Texas in 1974. "That beats on your head a little bit. I knew all the guys [in Milwaukee] from playing against them all those years. It was a great opportunity for me. (General manager) Harry Dalton was making a push. They were trying to do something special."

Eleven days before signing Howell, Dalton made a blockbuster trade with the St. Louis Cardinals, acquiring right-hander Pete Vuckovich, closer Rollie Fingers and catcher Ted Simmons. After learning of that deal, Howell knew the Brewers meant business. Thus, he signed with them knowing full well that veteran Don Money had been the club's third baseman for years.

Manager Buck Rodgers began platooning Money and Howell at third, often using the other to fill the designated hitter role. It was a new experience for Howell, a left-handed hitter who had become accustomed to playing on a regular basis. He played more than the right-handed-hitting Money, because there are more right-handed pitchers, but Howell struggled to a .238 average with only six homers and 33 RBIs in 76 games.

Howell's role changed again in 1982 when emerging star Paul Molitor was installed as the starting third baseman. Money and Howell were left to fend for at-bats almost exclusively at DH, a role which never felt quite right to the native Californian.

"It was definitely an adjustment, mentally and physically," said Howell. "It's not an easy thing to do. I always said it was like pinch-hitting four times. I stayed in the dugout between at-bats. There are things you can do on the bench to help your team.

"Don was a tremendous competitor and a really good hitter. I came to the ballpark every day, ready to play. Those were the circumstances. You fill your role and try to help win ballgames."

Trying to make the best of the situation, Howell enjoyed playing in a potent lineup that came to be known as "Harvey's Wallbangers" after Harvey Kuenn replaced Rodgers at manager in early June. The Brewers ravaged pitchers throughout the league, pounding 216 homers and scoring 891 runs. It was a sight to behold as the offense formed a conga line around the bases on a regular basis.

"One through nine, we had a lot of guys who could hurt you," said Howell. "There wasn't any place to take a breath in that lineup. They had to get all nine players out. We had one heck of a team, and everybody knew each other very well. It was a group of guys who knew how to play the game. There weren't many signs given. Guys knew what they were supposed to do. We had a lot of respect for each other. We played the game hard every day."

The Brewers played hard off the field as well, constantly pulling pranks on each other in a lively clubhouse. Coming up with Texas at age 20, Howell was accustomed to being the target of mischievous teammates. With the Brewers, however, he made sure he was on the other end whenever possible.

"It was all part of being big kids," he said. "You had to be careful. Payback can be a bitch. You just laid in the weeds and watched to see what was coming."

The Brewers' offense seldom rested but the pitching staff was in flux over the final weeks of the season. Fingers was lost to an arm injury, Moose Haas and Bob McClure were shifted to bullpen duty, and starting pitchers Doc Medich and Don Sutton were acquired from Texas and Houston, respectively. According to Howell, the glue that held it all together was Simmons, the savvy, intelligent veteran catcher.

"Teddy coming over, with his style and knowledge of hitters, was a big thing," said Howell. "We knew if we got on top late with Fingers, we were going to win. That's how it was. When you have somebody that dominant at the end, psychologically, it's a big thing. We missed that somewhat when he got hurt."

Howell still recalls the tenseness of the final day of the season in Baltimore, after the Brewers lost the first three games of the series to blow all of their three-game lead over the Orioles.

"Those first three games in Baltimore took the smile off your face," he recalled. "Emotions were up and down."

The Brewers prevailed in a big way in the final game, whipping Baltimore, 10-2. Howell started as the DH that day and contributed a run-scoring ground-out in two at-bats before yielding to Money. The roller-coaster ride continued in the ALCS against California when the Brewers lost the first two games before rallying to win three in a row to claim the pennant.

It was on to the World Series and an experience Howell never will forget.

"The biggest thing about it was the electricity, being able to play in the ultimate series," he said. "You could see the excitement in your teammates' eyes. Everybody was in it together. I think about it every day.

"When we were up 3-2, I don't think we ever doubted ourselves. We kept battling, did all we could."

It wasn't enough, however, as the Cardinals claimed the last two games at home to win the championship. The defeat was somewhat dispiriting on a personal level as well for Howell, who was held hitless in 11 at-bats by the St. Louis pitching staff.

"I hit in a little tough luck," he said. "You hit the ball hard and take your chances. It's not a good feeling left in your craw. I couldn't get the ball to get out of someone's glove. It can be a tough game. It was bad timing for me."

Howell played two more seasons with the Brewers before being released. The club was fading badly and dramatic personnel changes were being made. He signed with San Francisco but was released in spring training in 1985. He signed with Philadelphia and played that year in Triple-A, but Howell never would play another big-league game.

Howell did play one more year of ball in an unexpected turn. Like so many of his former Brewers teammates, he signed up for the Senior Professional Baseball Association in '89, playing for the St. Petersburg Pelicans. Howell batted .320 for the Pelicans, who went on to win the league's first and only championship. The senior circuit folded halfway through its second season.

Forced to get a real job, Howell started his own business, a financial service in San Luis Obispo, just down the road from his hometown of Lompoc. In 2000, he was offered a job as a minor league instructor by Simmons, his former teammate, who was running San Diego's farm system at the time. For six years, Howell served as a hitting coach and manager in the Padres' minor leagues.

"I really liked it," he said. "You try to help young players fulfill their dreams."

For the past two years, Howell has coached a college summer team. He also conducts youth baseball clinics, both in and outside the United States. His enthusiasm for baseball never wanes, and Howell takes every opportunity to pass on his expertise to those who yearn to follow his path and become big-league players.

"It's always in your blood," he said. "You find some capacity to keep doing it. It's people with a common interest in the game. We're all big kids. I don't care if you're 60 years old. That never leaves you. Nothing ever changes. Baseball is baseball."

Defining Moment
Splitting designated hitter duties with Don Money in 1982: "It was definitely an adjustment, mentally and physically."

Number to Remember
Howell batted .383 during a 14-game hitting streak in August of '82.

Favorite October Memory
Experiencing the excitement of being in the World Series: "The biggest thing about it was the electricity, being able to play in the ultimate series."

JAMIE EASTERLY

To this day, Gorman Thomas swears the only thing that kept him from completely losing his mind after being traded by the Brewers to Cleveland in 1983 was having teammate Jamie Easterly come with him.

"I don't know what I would have done without him," said Thomas. "He was my buddy."

Easterly and Thomas quickly became friends after the veteran left-handed reliever was acquired from Montreal near the end of the 1980 season. In a clubhouse full of pranksters, Easterly, known to teammates as "The Rat," and Thomas often could be found in the middle of the action.

"I liked to have fun," said Easterly, whose pronounced Texas drawl made him easy to pick out in a crowd. "We all kidded around with each other. It was a great bunch of guys to be around. Everybody had a good sense of humor. We could all laugh at ourselves. You had to on that team If you did something to somebody, you'd better be ready for revenge. You knew it was coming." Easterly also recalled closer Rollie Fingers being involved in the fun and games.

"I was kind of short, so Rollie called me 'a perfect circle,'" said Easterly. "He thought that was funny. I remember Rollie being in the middle of a lot of things. We used to get doughnuts and put them in his locker. I don't even remember why."

Nearly all of the Brewers were known by one nickname or another. Easterly wasn't particularly fond of his. So, how did he come to be known as "The Rat?"

"I played with this guy in Class A ball with the Braves in '71," he recalled. "I can't remember how to pronounce his name, but I thought he looked like Al Lewis on *The Munsters.* I called him 'Grandpa.' He said I looked like a rat.

"That made me mad, but it stayed with me. I've had it ever since. I thought it was derogatory, so I didn't like it. But once you get a nickname, it sticks with you. It bothered me for a long time, but it doesn't really bother me anymore. I still hear it every now and then."

Like many of his teammates, Easterly enjoyed the nightlife, hitting the bars for a drink or two or three. After one such evening during spring training in Sun City, Arizona, Easterly was late for the next morning's game of "flip," the daily take-no-prisoners competition in which players gathered in a circle and batted a baseball at each other with their gloves.

"We used to take roll on who was late," said Thomas. "All of a sudden, we look over and here comes Jamie wobbling down that ramp to the clubhouse."

"What happened?" asked Thomas.

"I lost my truck," replied Easterly.

"He had stopped to take a pee somewhere that night and forgot to get back in his truck," explained Thomas. "Somebody found it out in the desert three days later. He was a mess."

Easterly still insists you can't trust the veracity of any story Thomas tells, but you get the picture. The boys liked to have fun.

Easterly had a productive first year with the Brewers in '81. He pitched in 44 games out of the bullpen — a substantial number considering the season was shortened by a players' strike — compiling a 3-3 record and 3.19 ERA with four saves. He made two appearances in the Eastern Division Series against the New York Yankees, pitching a total of 1 1/3 innings.

Things didn't go nearly as well the following season, when the Brewers finally broke through to win the AL pennant and advance to the World Series. After making 22 appearances in the first half (3.75 ERA, two saves), Easterly was lost from July 12 until September 1 with a knee injury that required surgery.

"I had a knee problem early in my career with Atlanta, and they had shaved the bone down," said Easterly. "Over the years, it got irritated again, so they went back in there and cleaned it up. It was frustrating. You want to be part of the club when things are going good like that. The first part of the year I pitched halfway decent. I really wasn't even on the radar screen in the second half."

Easterly never recovered his form that season. In six September appearances, he was cuffed around for 12 hits and six runs in 6 2/3 innings. Those struggles made it easier for general manager Harry Dalton to leave Easterly off the club's post-season roster. Lefty Bob McClure was shifted from the rotation to the bullpen, and Fingers was kept on the roster despite being sidelined since Labor Day weekend with an arm injury.

"They kept Rollie on the roster, hoping his arm would come around," recalled Easterly. "He couldn't throw, but they did it anyway. I don't know if that kept me off the roster or not. I don't think I saw that coming. I wasn't throwing the ball all that well, but we all knew that Rollie had hurt his elbow. So, it was a bit of a surprise when that happened. I'm sure it was a tough decision for them.

"I never got to pitch in the World Series. I suited up and was kind of like a coach. I'd hit grounders to the infielders before the games. Then, I'd sit on the bench and watch. It was outstanding to be there. They didn't have to let me go to the games. But it still was a pretty big bummer not to pitch. Bob McClure did an outstanding job for us when they put him in the bullpen. You couldn't argue with that. But of course, I wanted to be in there.

"I would have loved to have thrown one pitch in the World Series. I wouldn't have cared how I did. Just to be able to say I pitched in the World Series would have been enough. But it wasn't meant to be."

Easterly had pitched in only 12 games for the Brewers in 1983 when informed on June 6 he had been traded with Thomas and minor leaguer Ernie Camacho to the Indians for center fielder Rick Manning and reliever Rick Waits. Thomas immediately went out and got drunk, setting the stage for a memorable TV interview that his former teammates still talk about.

"That one really knocked him in the dirt, so to speak," said Easterly. "He was a blue-collar type guy who always did the job and played hard. It was a pretty tough deal for him. It really devastated him.

"It seemed like after he got traded, every time he hit the ball hard somebody would catch it. He got so frustrated. One day he came in and tore off his jersey and said, 'I quit.' That trade took the fun out of it for him."

While Thomas was distraught over the trade, Easterly had a different perspective. He was closing in on the 10 years of big-league service needed for a full pension and was happy to still be in uniform, no matter what city was stitched across the front.

"I was in a different boat," he said. "I was just glad somebody picked me up and wanted me. I didn't like being traded from a World Series team to a last-place team, but I was glad they at least wanted me. I had some good years in Cleveland after I was traded."

Those years came to an end after the 1987 season, when the Indians released Easterly. He wasn't ready to quit. He just didn't have a choice.

"I didn't retire," he said. "Nobody wanted me."

Easterly joined many former Brewer teammates in Florida in 1989 to play in the short-lived Senior Professional Baseball League. He pitched for the Orlando Juice and had an offer from Clete Boyer to come to Bakersfield, California, the next year to play in a senior circuit that never got off the ground.

Easterly would never toe a pitching rubber again. He headed home to Crockett, Texas, where he had lived since age 8, to contemplate his next move.

"I had a 100-acre spread, but I didn't know anything about cows," he said with a laugh. "I let a friend use it for awhile for his cattle, but I eventually sold it."

Much to his surprise, Easterly soon entered the banking business, buying a small percentage of Citizens National Bank in Crockett. He still sits on the board of directors but indicated that gives him no special privileges.

"I can't walk in there and get money whenever I want," he said. "I wish I could."

Easterly and wife Stacy celebrated their 25th wedding anniversary this year. Their two children, Bryan and Michele, are in college. He plays a lot of golf, including some celebrity tournaments with old pal Thomas, eagerly anticipating the next time they'll see each other.

"We called Gorman 'Sybil' because he had about 15,000 personalities," said Easterly. "You never knew which one it would be from one day to the next."

Thomas, of course, had to have the last say, recalling one day on the road together with the Indians.

"We played an afternoon game and got back to the hotel late," said Thomas. "I had a room across the hall. I knocked on Jamie's door and walked in the room. He was on a dresser, with a lamp shade on his head, waiting to jump on me. I caught him in mid-flight and slammed him into the wall. That was after we had been kicked out of two bars."

Defining Moment

Easterly pitched in only six games after the All-Star break in '82 because of a knee injury that required surgery.

Number to Remember

Easterly pitched in 44 games for the Brewers in the strike-split season of 1981, compiling a 3.19 ERA with four saves.

Not-so-Favorite October Memory

Easterly was left off the post-season roster in 1982, denying him the chance to pitch in a World Series: "I would have loved to have thrown one pitch in the World Series. I wouldn't have cared how I did."

ROLLIE FINGERS

Even now, twenty five years later, whenever Rollie Fingers makes an appearance in Wisconsin or bumps into a Brewers fan along his travels, he hears some version of the same sentiment.

"They say, 'We wish you were healthy for the '82 World Series,'" Fingers said, somewhat ruefully.

"I always tell them, 'I wish I would have been healthy, too.'"

To this day, Brewers fans and those associated with the club at the time debate whether Fingers would have changed the course of franchise history that October. With Fingers sidelined with a torn muscle in his pitching arm, the Brewers battled the St. Louis Cardinals for seven games before bowing, 6-3, in the finale.

The Brewers led, 4-2, in the sixth inning of Game 2 before losing, 5-4. They had a 3-1 lead in the sixth inning of Game 7, only to watch the Cardinals rally to claim the title.

But that was the sixth inning, you say. What difference could a closer have made at that point of the game? Believe it or not, a late-inning reliever — the term "closer" wasn't in vogue yet — often would pitch two or three innings to finish a victory. It was years later when managers decided the ninth inning was the closer's domain, holding them back for the final three outs.

"I'd pitch two or three innings in a lot of my appearances," said Fingers. "You'd come in with the bases loaded, things like that. You didn't think anything of it. That's the way the game was played. You'd come into the game in the seventh inning and finish the game. I had the type of arm where I could go out and throw every day."

Fingers' rubber arm finally snapped on September 2, 1982, in the first game

In his first season with the Brewers in 1981, Fingers became the first relief pitcher in major league history to win both the Cy Young Award and Most Valuable Player honors.

of a doubleheader against Cleveland at County Stadium. With the Brewers clinging to a 2-1 lead, Fingers took over to start the eighth inning and struck out the side. But, while pitching to Mike Hargrove to open the ninth, Fingers felt something wrong in his forearm.

"It was a burning sensation," he recalled. "I didn't feel anything snap. It was just over the course of three or four pitches. It kept getting worse and worse. It wasn't any one particular pitch. It was a little sting at the beginning, then I got to about the fourth or fifth pitch and I said, 'That's it.' I knew it was something bad."

After fielding a sacrifice bunt by Toby Harrah, Fingers motioned to the dugout that something was wrong. He was removed from the game and examined by the team doctor, who thought it was nothing more than a strain.

Fingers was told to rest his arm for a week before trying to throw again. With the Brewers holding a slight lead in the AL East, it was the last thing Fingers wanted to hear, but he remained optimistic that he'd soon be back on the mound. He limited his activity for the next several days to shagging flies in the outfield during batting practice.

When Fingers finally tried to throw again in the bullpen and felt the same stinging sensation, he knew he was done.

"We only had three weeks left to go in the season," said Fingers. "They were hoping my arm would come around. They kept saying it was just a strain."

With Fingers sidelined, the Brewers relied on rookie Pete Ladd, who had been summoned from the minors at midseason, as well as Bob McClure, Jim Slaton and Dwight Bernard to finish games. That mix-and-match formula worked often enough for the Brewers to hold off Baltimore on the last day of the season to win the division, then stage a remarkable comeback from an 0-2 hole to win the best-of-five ALCS against California.

Hoping for a miraculous recovery by Fingers, general manager Harry Dalton and manager Harvey Kuenn decided to keep him on the active roster for the post-season. It would have been more beneficial to carry another healthy arm, but Fingers was the reigning AL MVP and Cy Young Award winner and the team's baseball bosses thought he deserved every opportunity to pitch if possible.

Before Game 1 of the World Series in St. Louis, Fingers threw to hitters in batting practice to test his arm.

"It didn't feel too bad," he recalled. "I went in and iced it and went down to the bullpen. I got up during the game to test it and it was still bad."

In the eighth inning of Game 4 at County Stadium, after the Brewers rallied for six runs in the seventh to take a 7-5 lead, Fingers actually got up in the bullpen. It was perceived by some as something of a decoy by Kuenn, but Fingers said nobody was fooled.

"St. Louis knew I hadn't been in a ball game in three or four weeks," said Fingers. "If you don't pitch after three or four weeks, you know something's wrong. Guys aren't that stupid. I couldn't pitch. It was just too sore. I may have made a difference. I may not have made a difference. I would have liked to at least have had the chance.

"They were trying just about everybody down in the bullpen. There were a couple of instances when I could have maybe come into a ball game and done something. We had the lead in Game 7. I'm sure if I had been healthy I would have pitched in that game. Not being able to play in the World Series was probably the low point of my career."

As it turned out, Fingers' injury was much worse than imagined. He was told to go home and rest over the winter, and he'd be as good as new the next spring. Much to his dismay, not to mention his teammates and club officials,

Fingers was not as good as new. Not even close.

"I tried pitching a couple of games there and it was just killing me," he said. "It turned out to be completely misdiagnosed. I had a torn muscle. I ended up having to have an operation and I missed the whole '83 season. What I should have done is have an operation right after the ('82) season. Then I would have been ready for '83. Instead, we waited and I missed the whole season."

Had Fingers pitched in 1983, the Brewers might have returned to the World Series. Ladd did an admirable job as his replacement, saving 25 games, but there was only one Rollie Fingers. Anyone who didn't think so must have been out of the country in 1981. Helping the Brewers finally make it to post-season play that year, Fingers put together a season unlike any other by a relief pitcher in major league history.

Though two months were lost to a union strike that resulted in a split season, Fingers barely had a hiccup. He led the majors with 28 saves, compiled a microscopic 1.04 ERA, walked only 13 batters in 78 innings while recording 61 strikeouts. In games he notched saves, the man with the handlebar moustache didn't allow an earned run, spanning 41 innings. Amazingly, Fingers allowed only one earned run all season at home.

Not only did Fingers claim the Rolaids Relief Man Award and Fireman of the Year, he was voted the unheard-of daily double of American League MVP and Cy Young Award.

"The funny thing about that year was the first game back after the strike was the All-Star Game in Cleveland and I got the loss," recalled Fingers. "Mike Schmidt hit a home run off me to win it.

"Other than that, it was one of those years when nothing went wrong. I could come in with the bases loaded and give up three line drives and they'd all be right at guys. It was one of those fantasy years. The guys made the plays behind me."

It was exactly what general manager Harry Dalton had in mind when he made the blockbuster trade with St. Louis in December 1980 that brought Fingers, right-hander Pete Vuckovich and catcher Ted Simmons to Milwaukee. Just four days prior to that trade, Fingers had been traded from San Diego to St. Louis. The next day, Cardinals general manager/manager Whitey Herzog acquired Bruce Sutter from Chicago, prompting the obvious question: What in the world was St. Louis going to do with two closers?

"Somebody asked, 'How are you guys going to get along together?'" recalled Fingers. "I said, 'I don't know if we're going to get enough work.' I knew something was going to happen. They would have to either trade Sutter or me somewhere."

Fingers returned home to San Diego to see what might happen. The next day, he picked up the newspaper and got the answer. The headline read: "Fingers traded to Milwaukee."

"That's how I found about it, in the paper," said Fingers. "I never got a call. I knew the Brewers needed a closer. They had tried several different guys. They had a great offensive ball club, scored a lot of runs. They just needed somebody to finish games out of the bullpen."

The Brewers knew they were getting a relief pitcher with an impeccable resume. Fingers was a key figure on the Oakland clubs that won three World Series in a row from 1972-'74, claiming MVP honors in the third conquest. During the '70s, he compiled 209 saves, 19 more than his closest challenger, Sparky Lyle.

"That first year we had Rollie, it was the best pitching I ever saw," said former second baseball Jim Gantner. "I only saw him throw one pitch down the middle all year, and he blamed me. We were in Boston and Rollie had the bases loaded with two outs. Darrell Evans was up with a 3-0 count and I was thinking, 'I hope he doesn't throw him a meat pitch right down the middle. Sure enough, he threw one and Evans hit a grand slam.

"After the game, I told Rollie, 'He's one of the best 3-0 hitters in the game.' He blamed me for the home run. He said, 'You should have come in and told me that. I'm new in the league.' He said, 'It's your fault he hit a grand slam. I could have just walked him and only cost us one run.'"

Fingers was enjoying another banner season in '82 until that fateful game against Cleveland on Labor Day weekend. After sitting out the following season, he made a strong showing with a bad club in 1984, notching 23 saves and compiling a 1.96 ERA in 33 appearances. Late that season, however, he ruptured a disc in his back pitching against the Yankees.

"They had to carry me out of bed the next morning," he said. "I couldn't even roll over. They had to scoop me out of bed, carry me downstairs and put me in an ambulance. I went to the hospital in Milwaukee and was there for a couple of days. They took some tests and saw the ruptured disc. I got on the plane to San Diego and had an operation the next day. The season was already shot."

Worried about Fingers' back, the Brewers signed him to an incentive-laden contract in 1985. Beyond his modest salary, he would receive $20,000 for each appearance.

"I pitched in 47 games and surprised them," he said. "They sat me down the last month of the season. They were definitely saving money and taking that out of my pocket. I was still under contract in 1986 and could have pitched for the Brewers, but (manager) George Bamberger didn't want me on the ball club. We didn't see eye to eye."

Fingers wasn't quite done with baseball. He signed on with the Senior Professional Baseball League in 1989 and pitched for the West Palm Beach Tropics, managed by former Boston skipper Dick Williams. The Tropics went 52-20, winning their division, but the league folded the next year.

Life changed forever for Fingers in 1992 when he was elected to the Baseball Hall of Fame in his second try on the ballot. He joined Hoyt Wilhelm, elected seven years earlier, as the only relief pitchers to make it to Cooperstown. They since have been joined by Dennis Eckersley and Bruce Sutter, but Fingers is still puzzled by the apparent bias against relievers by many of the Hall of Fame voters.

"I can't figure it out," said Fingers, who was the all-time saves leader with 341 at the time of his retirement. "I tell Goose Gossage every time I see him, 'You should have been elected six or seven years ago.' We pitched in the era where you pitched two or three innings, came in with the bases loaded, stuff like that. I was really the first true closer to go in. That was a real honor."

And, as Fingers accurately noted, "Once you get in the Hall of Fame, your life changes."

With a Cooperstown calling card, it was time to go into the Rollie Fingers business. He discovered money could be made, far easier than pitching during his time in the majors, by making personal appearances. Fingers dabbled in marketing for golf courses and the telecommunications business, but what he eventually settled on was being himself. He quickly discovered there was plenty of demand for Hall of Fame baseball players.

Fingers also plays golf on the Celebrity Players Tour, often with former Brewers teammate Gorman Thomas.

"I see Gorman quite a lot," he said. "We play five or six tournaments a year. We've been doing it since 1990. I've never won a tournament. I finished third once, a long time ago."

When not traveling around the country, Fingers is kept busy with his new family back home in Las Vegas. Beyond three grown children from previous marriages, he now has a 5-year-old son and 3-year-old daughter with wife Lori.

"I had a grandson born the same week as my son was born," Fingers said, shaking his head. "That keeps you young, especially in a two-story house when you're up and down the stairs 25 times a day. It keeps me in shape. You can't beat it."

One thing that hasn't changed is Fingers' trademark handlebar moustache, which he grew during his playing days in Oakland and never shaved.

"Reggie Jackson came to spring training with a moustache and wouldn't shave it off," recalled Fingers. "We started growing moustaches to get Reggie to shave his off. (Owner) Charlie Finley got wind of what we were doing and told everybody on the ball club that if we had a moustache on opening day, we'd get three hundred bucks. That's the only reason I did it."

And why a handlebar moustache?

"Just to be different," he said. "Everybody else was growing a regular moustache. Now, I'm stuck with it."

Rollie Fingers helped create a new look for men throughout Wisconsin in 1982. Here Fingers closely judges the Handlebar Moustache Contest prior to a game at County Stadium.

Defining Moment

In his first season with the Brewers in 1981, Fingers became the first relief pitcher in major league history to win both the Cy Young Award and Most Valuable Player honors.

Number to Remember

When Fingers retired in 1986, he was the major league's all-time leader with a total of 341 saves.

Not-so-Favorite October Memory

Fingers was not available to pitch in the post-season in '82 because of an arm injury suffered on Labor Day weekend: "Not being able to play in the World Series was probably the low point of my career."

BEN OGLIVIE

When Ben Oglivie instructs outfielders in the minor league system of the Tampa Bay Devil Rays, he always reminds them to be aware of their surroundings. It was a valuable lesson he learned on the final day of the 1982 season while carving a permanent niche in the Brewers' franchise lore.

"You always want to capture the moment," he said. "You shudder to think what might have happened otherwise."

In his accustomed spot in left field, Oglivie watched nervously as the Baltimore Orioles pushed a run across in the bottom of the eighth against Don Sutton to trim Milwaukee's lead to 5-2. After losing the first three games of the series, the Brewers had to win the season finale to avoid a total collapse and claim their first AL East crown.

"We went to Baltimore to win one game," said Oglivie. "We didn't want to have to win the last game. We wanted it to be the first game. It didn't work out that way."

With two down, Earl Weaver, who had announced it would be his last game as Baltimore's manager, sent left-handed hitter Joe Nolan to hit for Rich Dauer. Expecting Nolan to pull the ball, Oglivie shifted a couple of steps toward center. But, much to Oglivie's dismay, Nolan sent a slicing drive down the left-field line that had extra-base hit written all over it.

The wiry Oglivie knew there was little foul territory to negotiate between the line and the padded wall in that corner of Memorial Stadium. With little time to react, he raced over and went into a slide as he approached the stripe, reaching out to catch the ball just before it hit the ground. Oglivie then slid out of view of the TV cameras and smashed into the wall, causing Brewers fans back home to hold their breath. When he emerged with the ball, the inning was over and the 5-2 margin was safe.

The Brewers went on to score five runs in the ninth for a 10-2 victory that didn't tell the entire story of what might have been had Oglivie not made his fabulous catch.

"If he doesn't make that catch, the whole dynamics of the game at that point might change," said Mike Caldwell, the crafty Brewers left-hander who watched in amazement and relief from the visiting dugout. "That was a catch that a lot of average fans or non-baseball people might not even recognize. As far as that game went, that was a hell of a moment to make a hell of a catch. That took the wind right out of their sails."

Outfielders have scant time to plot their course of action on such plays. But Oglivie knew it was a tight corner and that a sliding catch was his only play.

"It was a dangerous corner," he called. "The space was limited. The line ran parallel to the wall, and it was very close. You just respond. It's more of an instinctive thing to go into a slide. I didn't expect him to hit it down the line. There's no way possible at the time to realize what you have done."

Now a coach with the Class A Vero Beach (Florida) Devil Rays, Oglivie realizes you can't teach instinct. But you can teach preparedness and awareness, especially when you're roaming the outfield in enemy territory.

"We teach these guys the same thing," said Oglivie. "You do your homework, get a feel for your surroundings. You have to have an idea. You can't say ahead of time, 'I'm going to slide.' You do whatever you can to catch the ball."

Oglivie was known more for his bat than glove, and rightfully so. Taking over in 1979 for injured Larry Hisle in left, he quickly emerged as one of the top sluggers in the league. In 1980, Oglivie batted .304, tied Reggie Jackson for the AL home run crown with 41 and drove in 119 runs. His home run total slipped to 14 in the strike-split '81 season, but he re-emerged in 1982 as one of the top run producers on the club (34 homers, 102 RBIs).

It is said that timing is everything in life, and that certainly was true for Oglivie when he was traded from Detroit to Milwaukee before the 1978 season for pitchers Jim Slaton and Rich Folkers. Slaton would re-sign with the Brewers the next year as a free agent, making that trade an absolute steal for general manager Harry Dalton.

"You don't understand what it means to be traded until it happens," said Oglivie, who had been dealt from Boston to Detroit for infielder Dick McAuliffe after the 1973 season. "When I got traded the second time, I understood what it meant. I had a chance to play more. It's a matter of maturing. When the door opens up, you have to take advantage of it. Who knows what would have happened if [Hisle] was healthy."

Oglivie arrived just as the Brewers were taking that last big step from pretender to contender. Anyone could look around and see there was a plethora of talent on hand. But what truly amazed the native of Panama was how well the players got along, on and off the field.

"People come together when they are interested in the other person," he said. "We did things outside the game. If you're not interested in the other person's life, there's not going to be openness. When you start feeling comfortable around people, it becomes a special time together. Coming to the ballpark early, doing different things in preparation for the game, brings you together. It was easy to talk to those guys.

"When I look at 1982, I think about the coming together of what it means to be a team. You can go through that process and not really see it at the time. That was the definition of what a team was. When you prepare a team for the future, that's the blueprint to use. You can look back at it now and see it. You don't realize at the time how it's evolving. I wasn't the center of it. I was just a part of it."

Like most of the players on that club, Oglivie was awarded a nickname by his teammates, like it or not. With a 6-2, 170-pound frame, he appeared to be all arms and legs, be it chasing after fly balls in the outfield or going sprawling into bases with what were known as crash-and-burn slides. Thus, Oglivie soon was known in the Brewers' clubhouse as "Spiderman."

"It was because of the unusual way I had of catching the ball," he said. "I had a way of stabbing the ball, like I was spinning something. And it stuck. I really didn't care. The intentions were good."

Maybe, maybe not.

"We called him 'Spiderman' because of his slides," said former second baseman Jim Gantner. "His arms and legs were going everywhere. He never slid the same way twice. He would invent new slides."

Oglivie firmly believes the togetherness of the '82 team helped the Brewers survive the harrowing final weekend in Baltimore. What was the mood that Saturday night as the Brewers tried to shake it off and get ready for the winner-take-all finale against the Orioles?

"I'd say confident yet concerned," recalled Oglivie. "I had a call that night from a friend. He said, 'Ben, what in the world is going on?' It wasn't a restful night at all. Sometimes, it looks like you've never played the game before. The beauty of baseball is you have the ability to come back the next day and try again. In less than 24 hours, we were getting ready to play another game."

Things didn't go nearly as well for Oglivie in the post-season. He banged up some ribs crashing into the outfield wall in Game 3 of the ALCS against California, opening the door for a new hero to emerge. Seldom-used Mark Brouhard started Game 4 and led the Brewers to a series-tying victory by going 3 for 4 with a home run, three RBIs and four runs scored.

Oglivie batted .133 in the ALCS, with one home run. He continued to struggle at the plate in the World Series against St. Louis, batting .222, again with just one homer. The Brewers' bats went cold up and down the lineup in the last two games in St. Louis, allowing the Cardinals to win both and come back to claim the title. Oglivie learned that fairy-tale endings sometimes are exactly that. Fairy tales.

"Our team had the confidence going in that we were going to win," he said. "It wasn't overconfidence. There are no excuses. The way that team came together, we thought we had the better team. But we didn't win. You move on. It wasn't meant to happen. We played our best. We didn't put our heads down. The guys gave it everything we had."

Oglivie learned to deal with a different kind of adversity in 1983. He missed long stretches of time with nagging shoulder and heel injuries, and his bat was badly missed. Oglivie played in only 15 games in September, when the team collapsed and quickly fell out of the race in the AL East after holding first place as late as August 25.

"When Benji came out of the lineup, that's when we fell out," recalled former catcher Ted Simmons. "He was a major contributor to our offensive production. I mean, major. When he stopped playing, so did we. That's how I remember that. It happened right then. We couldn't replace him."

One by one, injuries began to take their toll on other key players, including staff ace Pete Vuckovich and closer Rollie Fingers, and the Brewers' best days were behind them. In somewhat stunning fashion, the team slipped into a non-contending mode by 1984, and Oglivie knew major personnel changes were forthcoming.

"Unfortunately, that happens to every team," he said. "I can understand stuff like that now. People do get hurt. You can't plan for that. It's something that happens. It's part of the game. I was an integral part of the team. The pitchers were an integral part. Something changes, and it doesn't happen."

By the end of the 1986 season, it was Oglivie's time to go. His playing time was decreasing, and nagging injuries made it more difficult to be productive. Cut loose by the Brewers, he signed with the Kintetsu Buffaloes of the Japanese Pacific League, socking 46 home runs in his two years with that club.

Upon returning to the States, Oglivie was hired by the Brewers to do some instructing as well as scouting in the farm system. He now admits he was ill-prepared for the transition from player to coach.

"At the beginning, it's tough," he said. "You were a player, then you change gears. The first couple of years, I had no clue. You're teaching and I couldn't put it in words. I made some adjustments. I started writing things down, what I wanted to say. These guys have a short attention span, so you better be quick.

"My teaching is the part I struggle with. This isn't about me. This is about the game. This is about them. You draw out what each player does best. What can he give us? I deal with them individually. You want to bring out their talent and see them move to the next level. Development is primary. Nor that many make it, so development is the main thing, both as a person and a player."

After five years with the Brewers, Oglivie was hired by the Pittsburgh Pirates to be a hitting instructor in the minors. He worked in such places as Bradenton, Florida, Hickory, North Carolina, and Calgary, Alberta, Canada.

In 2000, Oglivie got his chance to return to the majors when the San Diego Padres hired him to be their hitting coach. Once again, adjustments had to be made to get the message across to big-league hitters.

"In the major leagues, there's not as much instruction," he said. "They need more reminding. They have already been taught. Players have to be ready to listen. You can't reinvent the game. There are no new fundamentals."

The Padres reassigned Oglivie to their farm system for the next five years, returning him to a familiar role. He accepted a similar job with Tampa Bay before the start of the 2007 season.

As for that exciting summer of 1982, Oglivie said, "I use that as a teaching tool now. You look back at past experiences. You can give a better picture to upcoming players, to show them what it takes to be a big league ballplayer, to be a good teammate. That was our year. It's something we can all relate to."

Defining Moment

Shutting down a Baltimore rally in the eighth inning with a remarkable sliding catch in the left-field corner on the final day of the '82 season: "You shudder to think what might have happened otherwise."

Number to Remember

Oglivie's 15 outfield assists in '82 ranked second in the American League to the Yankee's Dave Winfield (17).

Favorite October Memory

How hard the Brewers played in the post-season: "It wasn't meant to happen. We played our best. We didn't put our heads down. The guys gave it everything we had."

LARRY HISLE

Larry Hisle has spent much of his adult life counseling at-risk teenagers on the proper means of handling adversity. On that particular subject, he is uniquely qualified.

Making a simple throw from the outfield — something he had done hundreds of times without incident — Hisle saw a promising, productive major league career suddenly ruined. It happened on April 20, 1979, while playing left field for the Brewers against the Baltimore Orioles in Memorial Stadium.

"I remember that day like it was yesterday," said Hisle. "Mike Caldwell was pitching for us. When he pitched, I usually didn't get a lot of work. He had a great, sinking fastball, so there were not a lot of fly balls. But, on that particular night, I had four or five plays in left field in which I had to make hard throws."

It was the last throw that Hisle will never forget.

"It felt like someone stuck a knife in my shoulder," he said. "You think it's going to stop and the pain is going to go away. But it didn't."

Hisle soon learned he had torn the rotator cuff in his right shoulder. He traveled to Los Angeles to see noted sports orthopedist Frank Jobe, who recommended immediate surgery. But team doctors thought the injury might heal without surgery, so Hisle began a course of grueling physical therapy. He would play in only 26 games in 1979.

When his shoulder continued to pain him the following season, Hisle couldn't take it anymore. After playing in only 17 games, he underwent surgery in June, after which his shoulder was immobilized for four months.

"I had never gone through anything like that at all," he said. "I had a warped idea that a professional athlete would be protected from injury. There was no logic to it. That rehab was so hard. When they moved the shoulder one inch, it was the worst pain I ever felt. I accused the therapist of being a pro wrestler, he put my arm in so many positions. All the things I used to take for granted were impossible to do. I couldn't lift my arm over my shoulder."

Much to the dismay of Hisle, the shoulder was no better in 1981. An examination revealed the rotator cuff had torn again, and after playing in only 27 games, another season was shot. Almost a year to the day after his first surgery, he underwent yet another operation. Hisle was beginning to understand his career as a major league player was all but over.

"After the second surgery, the doctor recommended I never play again or risk losing use of the shoulder," he recalled. "I basically became left-handed. I did everything with my left hand."

The timing of Hisle's injury couldn't have been crueler. He signed with the Brewers as a free agent before the 1978 season, when the club was turning the corner from years of losing to emerge as a contender in the rugged AL East. In the strike-split season of '81, the Brewers finally made it to post-season play, bowing to the powerful New York Yankees in a hard-fought five game mini-playoff.

The Brewers broke through in a much bigger way in 1982, winning the division on the last day of the regular season in Baltimore, rallying from a 0-2 deficit to knock off California in the ALCS and battling St. Louis in a seven-game World Series that ended in disappointment. Hisle had become a full-time spectator by that October, calling it quits after a mere nine games.

"My dream was to play even after the two surgeries," he said. "I knew there would be a lot of difficulties and complications. I hoped the shoulder would allow me to get enough at-bats to make a contribution to my team."

The Brewers were fortunate to have a productive replacement in left field in Ben Oglivie, acquired in a trade with Detroit three weeks after Hisle signed as a free agent. The outfielders became friends, but that didn't ease the hurt of watching someone else take Hisle's place in the lineup.

"That bothered me a lot," admitted Hisle. "I thought I was going to be in left field a long time. Ben and I were good friends. It still was tough to see him run out to my position and play, even though he did an outstanding job. Most of that '82 season was doctors' appointments for me. I'd go to the ballpark and see the players. I didn't travel with the team. I was like everybody else in town, a fan."

With his dreams dashed of playing in the post-season, Hisle could barely watch as the Brewers took on the Angels and Cardinals. Sometimes, he sat in the stands at County Stadium and watched. Other times it was too painful and he went home to watch on television.

"I had mixed feelings," he said. "Sometimes I'd be really excited. Other times, I was disappointed. I was truly happy with what the team accomplished, but I couldn't get myself to believe I did anything to help them win. It was tough."

When Hisle arrived in 1978, the Brewers were coming off a 95-loss season, the eighth consecutive losing campaign since the club moved from Seattle to Milwaukee. But, under new manager George Bamberger, the Brewers broke through with 93 victories, the first step toward playing in the World Series four years later. Hisle played a key role in that turnaround, socking 34 home runs and driving in 115 runs for a power-packed lineup known as "Bambi's Bombers."

"To turn that around was almost a miracle," said Hisle. "We were competing against the likes of the Yankees, the Orioles and Red Sox. They were as good as any team in baseball. That was a difficult division. It was like a dream year for me. There was a lot of attention on free agents then, so there was a bit more pressure. I knew if I just focused on being myself, everything would take care of itself.

"I knew there would be times when everyone would be tested. I would try to say something positive to each player before every game. My job was to make sure they felt good about themselves. It was a wonderful experience. To go from that to not contributing at all was difficult to digest. It hurt a lot."

Though greatly discouraged by the premature end of his playing career, the Portsmouth, Ohio, native knew he had found a new home in Milwaukee. He and wife Sheila saw it as the perfect environment to raise son Larry Jr., who would later gain notice as a prep basketball star. After seven years out of the game, however, the elder Hisle began to get the baseball itch again.

"I made some calls and was hired by Toronto to be a hitting coach in the minor leagues," he said. "A couple of years later, they brought me to the big leagues."

Much to his surprise and delight, Hisle finally got to enjoy a World Series experience. The Blue Jays won consecutive championships in 1992 and 1993, with former Brewers teammate Paul Molitor leading the way the second time as World Series MVP.

"I call my second ring my 'Paul Molitor ring,'" said Hisle. "I don't know if we would have made it without him. I didn't think I'd ever make it to the World Series. I had put it out of mind. There's nothing like being in the World Series as a player. It would have been more enjoyable to participate in 1982. But it was still a great experience."

A few years later, Hisle would return to the Brewers, a development he never imagined. Another former Brewers teammate, Cecil Cooper, then running Milwaukee's farm system, invited him back as a minor league hitting coordinator. After one year in that job, however, Hisle decided it was time to hang up his baseball uniform for good.

"I had enough of the traveling," he said. "My son was at the age where I wanted to be home."

Hisle would soon find another productive role with the Brewers, this time off the field, joining the community relations department as Manager of Youth Outreach. Already engaged in youth activities with the local Boys and Girls Club and mentoring teenagers on the side, it was a perfect role for the soft-spoken former slugger who always had something positive to say. Having been adopted at age 15, Hisle knew the obstacles and temptations many teenagers faced, particularly those in difficult family environs.

"I still remember the first kid I worked with," he recalled. "He had been kicked out of the house by his mother. He was a horrible student. But he eventually became a good athlete and his mother took him back in. I was disappointed the day his mother called and said they were moving to Atlanta. I knew I was going to miss watching him grow."

Harking back to those devastating days after his throwing shoulder came apart, Hisle added, "Having to overcome that helped me empathize with the challenges these kids go through on a daily basis. I work with kids who present some of the most difficult challenges I've ever dealt with.

"It has been so rewarding, even to this day. I found that I can connect with these kids. To me, it's the biggest benefit of having been a professional athlete. They remember who I am and what I've done, and it allows me to reach out to them. There's no greater joy than to see kids turn their lives around. I found my calling in life."

Defining Moment

On April 29, 1979, Hisle suffered a torn rotator cuff making a throw from left field in Baltimore: "You think it's going to stop and the pain is going to go away. But it didn't."

Number to Remember

In his first and only full season with the Brewers in 1978, Hisle compiled a .533 slugging percentage, with 24 doubles and 34 home runs.

Favorite October Memory

As hitting coach for the Toronto Blue Jays in 1992 and 1993, Hisle received two World Series rings: "It would have been more enjoyable to participate in 1982."

PAUL MOLITOR

Paul Molitor can't help wondering if the fate of the Brewers in the 1982 World Series might have changed if only he had heard Robin Yount whistle.

It was the sixth inning of Game 7 in St. Louis, and the Brewers were clinging to a 3-1 lead over the Cardinals with ace Pete Vuckovich on the mound. With one down, Ozzie Smith singled to left, bringing Lonnie Smith to the plate.

Playing third base, Molitor did not have the proper angle to see what pitches catcher Ted Simmons was calling. But the Brewers were a veteran team always looking for an edge, and Yount often relayed pitches to Molitor from his post at shortstop, where he could see what finger Simmons was putting down.

"Robin would try to indicate pitches to me, to help me understand when he was shading in the hole," explained Molitor. "On that particular pitch, Robin had given me a heads-up for an off-speed pitch, which meant I'd normally shade the line a little more. I already was playing in because Lonnie Smith was a fast runner."

There was one problem, however. Because of the crowd noise at Busch Stadium, Molitor didn't hear Yount, so he stayed where he was, off the line. Smith pulled the breaking pitch from Vuckovich down the line, past the diving Molitor and into the corner for a double, putting two runners in scoring position. Manager Harvey Kuenn replaced Vuckovich with lefty Bob McClure, the Cardinals went on to score three runs and eventually claimed the championship with a 6-3 victory.

"That was a small thing, but if I had been cheating a bit toward the line, it might have made the difference," said Molitor. "That was the rally that turned the game. I've never watched Game 7 on TV. I'd like to see if I had cheated over if it would have made a difference. That [artificial] turf was fast. That's one of the idiosyncrasies of the game."

The discouraging ending to the '82 World Series was in stark contrast to how it began for Molitor and the Brewers. Known as "The Igniter" for his role atop a high-powered offense, Molitor touched off a 10-0 rout in Game 1 by collecting five hits. He wasn't aware he had made World Series history until walking out to his position in the bottom of the ninth inning.

"I remember looking up at the message board and seeing 'Paul Molitor became the first player in World Series history to get five hits in a single game,'" he recalled. "It just kind of hits you. You don't stop to think that no one had ever done it before. It wasn't very pretty. Five singles. Ozzie dove and knocked down three of them at short and almost threw me out on two of them. It was a heck of way to have your first World Series game unfold.

"Robin was batting behind me and had four hits, so we had nine hits in the top two spots in the lineup. It was a great start. The way we had gotten there, winning the last game of the season in Baltimore, coming back to win the last three games against California (in the ALCS) and then to have a 'breather' game to start, I think a lot of us felt we were destined to win. I don't know if inexperience as a player caused me to get ahead of myself, but I was feeling good about our chances."

A World Series title was not meant to be, but Molitor still gets goose bumps when recounting that glorious fall for the Brewers, particularly the historic comeback against the Angels. Like many of his teammates, Molitor can't remember County Stadium being any louder than in Game 5 of the ALCS, particularly after Cecil Cooper gave the Brewers the lead, 4-3, with a two-run single in the seventh inning.

"I'd heard County Stadium get loud before," said Molitor. "But I can honestly say there was a distinct difference in what that place sounded like after Cecil got that hit. It felt like it was vibrating, and with that facility, it probably actually was. It was something pretty special."

As uplifting as that experience was, Molitor still remembers the silent plane ride home from St. Louis after dropping Game 7 to the Cardinals. It was little consolation that the Brewers battled to the very end, as they always did. The team had been built to win that season, and to a man, each player realized what had slipped away.

"That night was tough," recalled Molitor. "I remember weeping to some degree, trying to deal with the disappointment. On the plane, everybody was trying to console each other. But it was a pretty depressing flight. Having witnessed the celebration and the [police] horses on the field in St. Louis, and everything that went with it, it wasn't easy."

The players were surprised to learn that plans for a parade through

Milwaukee the next day remained intact, despite the disheartening defeat. Most anticipated the event with dread, still trying to get over the heartbreak that was only a few hours old. Yet, to their surprise, the city turned out in unexpected numbers, creating a celebration every bit as vibrant as the one feting the winners back in St. Louis.

"I was not surprised at all that we had a great turnout because of the love affair between that city and that team," said Molitor. "I didn't know exactly how it would play out, but I thought the people would still want to express their gratitude. I was kind of a realist that even though we didn't win, it was probably the right thing to do.

"I remember saying after the parade that judging by the reaction of the crowd you wouldn't have known if we had won or lost. It turned out to be a nice pick-me-up for everybody. It was a beautiful fall day. It was cool but nice, the sun was out."

Already in his fifth season with the Brewers in '82, Molitor overcame a couple of injury-plagued years to play in 160 games. He joined Yount (210) and Cooper (205) in the 200-hit club with 201, marking the first time since the 1915 Detroit Tigers that three teammates reached the plateau in the same season. Molitor led the AL with 136 runs scored, the highest total since Boston icon Ted Williams crossed the plate 150 times in 1949.

"When you think about it, I scored about half the times I got on base that year," said Molitor, who replaced the veteran tandem of Don Money and Roy

Known as "The Ignitor," Molitor joined Robin Yount (210) and Cecil Cooper (205) in the 200-hit club in 1982 with 201. It was the first time since the 1915 Detroit Tigers that three teammates reached the plateau in the same season.

Howell at third base. "I got on base about 270 times, roughly, and scored 136 runs. How many guys score half the time they're on base? Being at the top of a lineup where the MVP (Yount) is hitting second and Cecil Cooper was batting third, you're going to score a lot of runs."

Molitor was not surprised that the Brewers took off that season after Kuenn moved from hitting coach to replace manager Buck Rodgers on June 2. With a veteran-laden club that knew how to play the game, Kuenn basically sat back and stayed out of the way, a different approach from the hands-on style of Rodgers.

"Harvey could pretty much write out the same lineup on a regular basis," said Molitor. "He had the perfect personality for the club because it didn't need a lot of 'overmanaging.' I liked Buck, but it was his first time through. He was a little rigid. He might have wanted to establish himself, and that's how he managed. It just wasn't a team that needed that. He proved to be successful later. It just wasn't working with that club."

The club known as "Harvey's Wallbangers" was not destined to remain intact for long, however. After the team faded down the stretch in 1983, Kuenn was dismissed and general manager Harry Dalton began turning over personnel. The championship window had slammed shut on the Brewers, something few players saw coming.

"We went from first to fifth in a very short time at the end of that season," recalled Molitor, whose batting average dropped to .270 as he battled through a wrist injury. "It went downhill very quickly. It was a veteran team. That tells you that with age and different things, it wasn't going to last too long. That club was set up to have a chance to win for a short time."

After a few tough years, the Brewers bounced back in 1987 with an unpredictable club known as "Team Streak." Shortly after jumping out to a record 13-0 start, the Brewers lost 12 in a row, setting the stage for a rollercoaster season full of ups and downs. Molitor got in the streaking spirit in the second half with a franchise-record 39-game hitting streak, seventh-longest in major league history. That streak ended on August 26 with Molitor on deck as Rick Manning delivered the game-winning hit in the 10th inning against Cleveland, prompting the fans at County Stadium to boo their own player.

"I always felt bad for him about that," said Molitor, who batted a career-high .353 that season. "You don't see a guy get booed at home very often for winning a game."

In an effort to put a series of injury-plagued seasons in the rear-view mirror, Molitor eventually settled into the designated hitter role, a natural progression for a player born to hit. Realizing it would extend his career, Molitor came to accept that evolution, and continued to pound out the base hits.

In what became a painful experience for Molitor, the club and its fans, his 15-year tenure in Milwaukee came to an end after the 1992 season. Trying to control the bottom line in a turbulent time for small-market franchises, team president Bud Selig and general manager Sal Bando, a former Brewers teammate, allowed Molitor to leave as a free agent for Toronto. Each side blamed the other for the ugly separation, and it would take years for Molitor and the Brewers to reconcile.

"Bud and Sal and I have all made our peace with each other," said Molitor. "I think they were disappointed in some things I did, and I was certainly disappointed in the way they handled some things. They didn't really give me much of a choice. That's not blaming anyone. It's just the way it was. It was the beginning of the separation of low-revenue and high-revenue markets."

The exodus came with one immediate bonus. While the Brewers spiraled into a non-competitive mode, Molitor was able to experience the World Series again - and this time with a more enjoyable ending. Toronto defeated the Philadelphia Phillies to win the title for the second consecutive year, with Molitor playing a significant role as World Series MVP. It was a watershed moment for Molitor, who proved beyond a shadow of a doubt he was a prime-time player.

"I always had hoped to be like Robin and end my career as a Brewer," said Molitor. "You play somewhere 15 years and you can't imagine going anywhere else. But I was able to get back to the World Series, 11 years removed from '82.

"There was a strong intent on my part to savor the visual pictures of that second time because the first one had become kind of a blur. You're younger back then and you think you're going to go back. I was able to really slow it down in terms of performance and also enjoyment."

Molitor's career would take yet another fateful turn in 1996 when the Twin Cities native returned home to play for Minnesota. Proving there was plenty of gas left in his tank as he reached age 40, Molitor established a career high with 225 hits, including magic No. 3,000 on September 16 in Kansas City, a triple, no less.

"If I hadn't gone to Toronto I probably wouldn't have had the chance to go back home to Minnesota," said Molitor, who turned down an offer to rejoin the Brewers. "I kind of went full circle. A few reasons stuck out. My dad was able to get in his car and see me play and not have to fly. That was really nice. He got to see me play more games those last three years than he had the previous 18 years."

Molitor retired after the 1998 season, and his number "4" was retired by the Brewers the next year. During his speech that day in ceremonies at County Stadium, he announced that should he be elected to the Hall of Fame — a no-brainer that came true in 2004 — he would go in as a Milwaukee Brewer. Any bitterness over his departure in '93 vanished that day, an appropriate salute to one of the greatest players in franchise history.

"Going into the Hall of Fame as a Brewer was a slam dunk," he said. "I never had any other thoughts. The Brewers retired my number and it kind of brought closure to the negativity. I still get goose bumps when I see my number hanging up there in Miller Park. It's pretty amazing."

Remaining in Minnesota after retiring, Molitor kept his hand in the game. For two years, he was bench coach for Twins manager Tom Kelly, before settling into a role as a minor league instructor in the organization. He went to Seattle in 2004 to serve as hitting coach for the Mariners before returning to resume instructing Minnesota's minor leaguers. The flexibility of that job allows him to spend more time at home with second wife Destini and their children, Julia, 3, and Benjamin, 1. Blair, a daughter from his previous marriage, graduated this year with honors from the University of Southern California.

"I'm 50 years old and I've got two little kids at home, so it's rejuvenating," he said. "God has been good to me, has given me a second chance. Things are good. With my job, I have time to spend with my family and also my non-profit work (including the Strike Out Cancer program). Those are things that bring me pleasure.

"I still need my baseball fix. I love teaching the kids. It took me a while to get comfortable with it and being a little more vocal, but they listen. The farther you're removed from playing, the less they know about you. You have to earn your credibility every year by giving them something that helps them. I think I'll keep doing it for a little while longer."

Defining Moment

Molitor set a World Series record in his very first game by collecting five hits in Game 1 in St. Louis.

Number to Remember

Molitor scored 136 runs in 1982, the most since Boston's Ted Williams scored 150 in 1949.

Favorite October Memory

Listening to the crowd noise after Cecil Cooper put the Brewers ahead with a two-run single in Game 5 of the ALCS against California: "It felt like it was vibrating, and with that facility, it probably actually was."

ROBIN YOUNT

When Robin Yount awoke on the morning of October 21, 1982, he was in no mood to party. The Brewers had lost Game 7 of the World Series the previous evening in St. Louis, and the soon-to-be American League Most Valuable Player was heartbroken.

The last thing Yount wanted to do was be part of the parade through downtown Milwaukee, scheduled to take place even though the Brewers came home without the trophy. The day's festivities were to conclude at County Stadium with a rally saluting the city's beloved "Harvey's Wallbangers."

Much to the surprise of players and club officials, the parade did turn out to be a raucous celebration, with people lined five-deep along Wisconsin Avenue to applaud the AL champs. But the best moment was yet to come, for those who ventured to the ballpark for the closing ceremony.

With some 20,000 cheering fans in the stands, the players were introduced, one by one, walking onto the field. When Yount's name was announced, however, he was nowhere to be found. Suddenly, the bullpen gate swung open and out roared a leather-clad rider on a motorcycle, one fist raised in the air. When the crowd realized it was Yount, they went nuts, screaming their approval.

Soaking up the moment, Yount took a lap around the outfield warning track and raced to home plate, slamming on the brakes and dismounting. At that instant, a legend was born.

Yount, who had ridden motorcycles since his early years as a teenager, never imagined his stunt would become a part of franchise lore. He viewed it as more of a cathartic event, a means of soothing the extreme disappointment of losing a World Series that every player on the team thought they should have won.

"I was being sort of rebellious," Yount recalled. "I was in a mood that I didn't care about anything. The last thing I wanted to do was go to that parade. It turned out to be a great event. It made us feel like we won it."

The only person not expressing his approval was stunned club president Bud Selig, who closed his eyes and prayed that one of his most valuable commodities would not crash in front of his very eyes.

"I almost had a heart attack," said Selig.

As it turned out, Yount's unforgettable ride was the result of a dare from three teammates, Pete Vuckovich, Ted Simmons and Gorman Thomas. When they saw the unlicensed motorcycle parked in the tunnel under County Stadium, they coaxed Yount to ride it onto the field during introductions. At first, he balked at the idea. But his teammates wouldn't relent, and the normally understated Yount decided to go for it.

"It was out of character," he admitted. "It wasn't even a street-legal bike. Those guys egged me on to do it. The next thing I knew, I was riding it out on the field. It turned out to be fun for everybody. I guess it's something that people remember."

It was a fitting culmination of a year to remember, for Yount and the Brewers. Already in his ninth season in Milwaukee at age 26, Yount burst onto the national scene with a dynamic performance in which he led the majors with 210 hits, 367 total bases, a .578 slugging percentage and 46 doubles. He was the first shortstop to lead the league in slugging and total bases, finishing with a .331 batting average, 29 home runs and 114 RBIs.

During the Brewers' final home stand, chants of "MVP! MVP!" often rang out from the stands at County Stadium, a prophecy that came true during the off-season.

"I do remember the fans chanting that," said Yount, known throughout his career as "The Kid" after breaking in as a scrawny 18-year-old rookie in 1974. "To say I wasn't aware of it, I'd be lying. But that wasn't the focus for me. I could care less, one way or the other, as long as we kept winning. With what we were going through the last two weeks, every game was so important. (Being MVP) certainly wasn't anything I considered."

Before the year was over, Yount would add a Silver Slugger and Gold Glove to his collection of awards. He rose to the occasion when needed throughout the season, but never more so than the final day in Baltimore, when the Brewers had to win or go home. Yount slugged home runs in his first two at-bats against future Hall of Famer Jim Palmer, sparking the Brewers to a 10-2 victory over the Orioles and their first AL East crown.

Yount's bat was quiet (.250, no RBIs) in the come-from-behind triumph over California, but he got it going again in the World Series, beginning with the first of two four-hit performances in Game 1. A team player throughout his 20 years with the Brewers, Yount's personal achievements meant little after the

In 1982 Yount became the first shortstop to lead the league in slugging and total bases, finishing with a .331 batting average, 29 home runs, and 114 RBIs. He was named the '82 American League MVP.

Cardinals came back to win the last two games and claim the title.

"Every athlete wonders what he will perform like on center stage," said Yount. "Until you get a chance, you never know. To play halfway decent was gratifying. But I'd take a 0-for-20 if we had won the championship. I can promise you that.

"For me, personally, I played that nutty game for 20 years. I played in one World Series. That's the goal, to play in the World Series. It was always my main focus. I never got to play in another one. When you get that close, it certainly hurts. I wouldn't trade playing in one and losing for not playing in one at all.

"The highlight of my career was playing in the World Series. Not to win it also hurt more than anything else, especially when I never got another shot. Never in my wildest dreams did I think I'd never see another one. We had so much going for us. I just assumed we would get another shot. But it doesn't work out that way. It's not that easy."

A late fade in '83 was the precursor of several dark years for the Brewers as Yount watched one teammate after another depart. He desperately yearned to get back to the World Series, to the point of strongly considering leaving the club as a free agent a few years later. To this day, he has trouble reconciling the fact in his mind that it was one-and-done for the franchise, as far as the World Series was concerned.

"All I remember about '83 was getting off to a bad start (the Brewers were eight games out in late June)," he said. "Then we made a legitimate run at it and got in first place. We shot every bullet we had in our arsenal to get there. When we got to the home stretch, we had nothing left. We hit the wall.

"In hindsight, we peaked in '82 as a team. That group of guys peaked. I would never have believed that would happen. That division was so good. Some years, we'd finish with a great record and be in third place. All but that one year."

Yount continued to produce offensively, but his career took an unexpected turn when a series of shoulder problems forced him to abandon shortstop and move to center field. Undaunted, Yount turned himself into the best center fielder he could be, making a memorable diving catch for the final out of Juan Nieves' no-hitter in Baltimore on April 15, 1987, one of the highlights of the Brewers' record 13-0 start that season.

In 1989, after the Brewers made a late run at the AL East lead before dropping back and finishing at .500, Yount claimed his second MVP Award. He batted .318 with 21 home runs and 103 RBIs, joining the legendary Stan Musial and Hank Greenberg as the only major leaguers to win MVP trophies at two positions. Somewhat surprisingly, Yount ranks that performance above his heroics in '82, in large part because the Brewers' lineup was not nearly as potent.

"I thought the best year I ever had was 1989," he said. "I say that because we didn't have a great team that year. My numbers might have been better in '82, but the supporting cast was so good. Not that we didn't have good players in '89. I just thought I hit the ball better that year. Offensively, I thought I had the best year of my career.

"That offense we had in '82 was amazing. It might have been in the top 10 in all of baseball history. Player for player, we had the same kind of team the Yankees had in their great years."

For Yount, the personal highlights kept coming. He collected his 3,000th career hit on September 9, 1992, an opposite-field single off Cleveland's Jose Mesa on an electrified night at County Stadium. He played one more season for the Brewers, making it an even 20 before hanging up his spikes. Yount had become the face of the franchise, an icon known as much for his unselfish style of play as any individual achievement.

"A lot of good players came through those teams, especially in the late '70s and early '80s," said Bob Uecker, the longtime radio voice of the Brewers who became extremely close with Yount. "But there's always got to be a 'base' guy. That guy was Robin. When you look at what he did back then, especially as a shortstop, he was pretty damn good. There's a lot of good shortstops today, no doubt, but to be as consistent as Robin was, day after day, that's saying something."

That consistency was rewarded in ultimate fashion in 1999 when Yount was elected to the Baseball Hall of Fame on the first ballot. He became the first player to enter the hallowed halls of Cooperstown representing the Brewers, five years after the club retired his now-famous No. 19. During an impressive induction speech, Yount expressed how grateful he was to spend 20 years as "The Kid," playing the game he loved in Milwaukee.

"It's been a great dream," he told the massive audience that came that day to the remote village in upstate New York to watch Yount, good friend George Brett and Nolan Ryan officially join the game's elite. "But if in fact this is reality, then with all due respect, Mr. Gehrig, today I consider myself the luckiest man on the face of the earth."

Determined to derive as much pleasure from retirement as in his two decades with the Brewers, Yount has remained true to his greatest loves - family, baseball and motorsports. For a time, he was part-owner of a race team in the Champ Car Atlantic Series, though he would rather have been in the cockpit than on the sidelines. In fact, to help quench his need for speed, Yount took the racing equivalent of a driver's education course in California.

It was back to the baseball diamond in 2002 when Yount accepted a position as first base coach for the Arizona Diamondbacks, his hometown team. He later served as bench coach, but in keeping with the high principles he has used to guide his life, Yount resigned out of loyalty in 2004 when manager Bob Brenly was dismissed.

After much pleading, coercing and cajoling from manager Ned Yost, Yount finally returned to the Brewers in 2006 as bench coach. His homecoming was a momentous occasion for the franchise but, sadly, a short one. After just one season, Yount decided family ties were more important, and reluctantly left the Brewers once again.

At some point, might we see Yount back in a baseball uniform again?

"I've retired three times," joked Yount. "I don't know the answer to that. I can say it won't be in any other uniform than the Brewers. I'll always have fond feelings for the Brewers. I don't know if they'll have me back. I loved that job. It was just hard living in a hotel for six months. That's the hardest part.

"My heart is still in baseball. It's what I know best. I still feel most comfort-

"A lot of good players came through those teams in the late '70s and early '80s. But there's always got to be a 'base' guy. That guy was Robin. When you look at what he did back then, especially as a shortstop, he was pretty damn good." -Bob Uecker

able in a baseball uniform. I have an extreme love for both baseball and motor sports. I have fun in both. How can you beat it? I'm the luckiest guy in the world. I feel like all I've ever done in my life is played."

Inheriting that love of baseball from his father, Dustin Yount played six seasons in Baltimore's farm system before latching on this year with the St. Joe, Missouri, Blacksnakes of the independent American Association.

"He loves to play more than I did," said Robin. "He'll keep playing until they rip the uniform off him. Why not? He's having fun. I told him it beats working for a living."

With daughters Melisa, Amy and Jenna as well as Dustin out of the house, Yount and wife Michele are empty nesters these days. But Yount is no less active, filling his days with physical activities whenever possible, including riding motorcycles. Which raises the question: What ever happened to that motorcycle he rode into County Stadium on that crisp autumn day in 1982?

"I sold that to somebody shortly after that, I think," said Yount, somewhat fuzzy about the transaction. "I might have gotten rid of it that winter. I never thought of it as being a historic piece."

But, as longtime Brewers fans will attest, it most certainly was.

Defining Moment

Yount's breakthrough performance in 1982 earned him the first of his two American League Most Valuable Player awards.

Number to Remember

Yount topped the major leagues with a .578 slugging percentage in 1982.

Favorite October Memory

Getting the chance to play in one World Series, even if it ended in defeat: "I wouldn't trade playing in one and losing for not playing in one at all."

THE OTHERS

During any given season, players come and go on every team, often making only cameo appearances. Some return the next season, others are never heard from again. It's all part of the ebb and flow of a 162-game major league season.

Kevin Bass, Bob Skube, Doug Jones and Chuck Porter all played for the Brewers during the glorious summer of 1982. If you blinked, you might have missed them. But they were all there, if only for brief periods.

Bass, a highly regarded young outfielder, and Jones, a reliever trying to make that final step after a couple of seasons with Class AAA Vancouver, came north with the club at the end of spring training. Neither stayed for long.

After only 18 games and nine at-bats without a hit, Bass was returned to Vancouver in mid-May when reserve infielder Rob Picciolo was acquired from Oakland. Later that year, on August 30 to be exact, Bass was the key figure on the Brewers' end in the trade with Houston for right-hander Don Sutton, the starting pitcher who put the club over the top and won the division-clinching game in Baltimore on the final day of the season.

Jones, who made his major league debut on April 9 with a scoreless inning of relief against Toronto, pitched only four times (10.15 ERA) before going back to Vancouver when veteran right-hander Jim Slaton came off the disabled list. Injuries sidetracked Jones' career and he was released by the Brewers after the 1984 season.

After his debut in '82, it would be 14 years before Jones would wear a Brewers uniform again. In a well-traveled career that took him through Cleveland, Houston, Philadelphia, Baltimore and Chicago, he was released by the Cubs in June 1996 and signed by the Brewers. The next year, in one of the more remarkable seasons ever by a Milwaukee relief pitcher, Jones set club records with 36 saves and 25 in a row during one stretch. In 75 appearances, the change-up specialist compiled a 2.02 ERA. Jones, who was 35 at the time, would go on to pitch three more seasons, including a return to Cleveland and a final stop in Oakland. He pitched in 846 games and accumulated 303 saves.

Skube and Porter saw action at the other end of the '82 season as September call-ups. Skube, who collected his first big-league hit on September 17 against the Yankees, was used as a pinch-hitter three times (two hits) and a defensive replacement in center once. He appeared in 12 more games with the Brewers in

1983, completing his very brief career in the majors. This year, Skube is serving as hitting coach for San Diego's Class A Fort Wayne affiliate in the Midwest League.

Porter, a starting pitcher in the minors who appeared in 25 games for Vancouver in '82, was added to the roster in September to provide another arm in the bullpen. He saw action in only three games, including both ends of the doubleheader sweep by the Orioles in Baltimore on the final Friday of the season. The Brewers would lose the next day as well, forcing them to win behind Sutton in Game No. 162 to avoid a horrible collapse.

Porter pitched in the Brewers' starting rotation in 1983 but blew out his elbow the following season and underwent "Tommy John" reconstructive surgery. He pitched in only six games for the Brewers in 1985, signaling the end of his major league career.

BACK ROW: Rob Picciolo, Ben Oglivie, Pete Vuckovich, Gorman Thomas, Randy Lerch, Rollie Fingers, Dwight Bernard, Robin Yount and Ned Yost.
THIRD ROW: Clubhouse Attendant Tony Migliaccio, Ted Simmons, Moose Haas, Paul Molitor, Don Money, Mike Caldwell, Mark Brouhard, Jerry Augustine & Jim Slaton.
SECOND ROW: Trainer John Adam, Visiting Clubhouse Manager Jim Ksicinski, Marshall Edwards, Roy Howell, Ed Romero, Bob McClure, Charlie Moore, Jamie Easterly, Vice President Tom Ferguson and Trainer Freddie Frederico.
FIRST ROW: Jim Gantner, Coaches Pat Dobson and Harry Warner, Manager Harvey Kuenn, Coaches Ron Hansen and Larry Haney and Cecil Cooper.
FRONT ROW: Bat Boys: Bob Vitale, Bill Zito, Steve Froemming, Jim Topitzes and John Booker.
Missing from Photo: Coach Cal McLish, Clubhouse Attendant Chris Sampson

THE RIGHT MAN

In many ways, Harvey Kuenn was destined to manage the Brewers. Born in West Allis, Wisconsin, a suburb of Milwaukee, he was a "cheeser" through and through.

Kuenn attended Milwaukee Lutheran High School and the University of Wisconsin, where he played both basketball and baseball. After signing a big bonus in 1952 with the Detroit Tigers, he needed only one minor league season to get ready for the big leagues.

In his first full season with the Tigers, Kuenn batted .308 and led the majors with 209 hits. Starting at shortstop for Detroit for seven years, he batted below .300 just once. After leading the American League with a .359 average in 1959, Kuenn was traded to Cleveland for home run champ Rocky Colavito in a stunning deal. Over 15 big-league seasons, he carried a .303 average.

In other words, Kuenn knew hitting. Accordingly, it was no shock when Brewers owner Bud Selig brought Kuenn back home to Milwaukee in 1971 to be a spring training and minor league instructor. By the next year, he was the team's hitting coach.

Despite ongoing health problems that included heart surgery in 1976, a stomach operation the following year and the amputation of his right leg below the knee in 1980, you couldn't keep Kuenn down. A down-to-earth Midwesterner conspicuous only by the gargantuan chaw of tobacco inside his cheek, Kuenn was loyal to the players, who over time grew to love him.

Kuenn and wife Audrey ran a bar/motel in West Allis called Cesar's, and players often dropped by for a beer or two. It also was a popular watering hole for the team's fans, who treated the Kuenns like royalty.

"We had a special relationship with Harvey," said Mike Caldwell, a veteran left-hander who spent eight years with the Brewers. "We were all fond of Harvey. Guys used to mess around with him all the time."

Nothing was sacred in a clubhouse full of devilish pranksters, including Kuenn's prosthetic leg. He would take it off to go into the shower, and when he emerged, it wasn't always where he left it.

"Gorman loved to hide it," recalled Caldwell. "He used to hide that son of a bitch once a home stand. Harvey would laugh about it, but I'm sure it pissed him off at times."

No player was closer to Kuenn than Robin Yount, who arrived in the big leagues in 1974 as a raw, gawky 18-year-old shortstop. As time passed, Yount discovered that his somewhat unorthodox batting style was similar to Kuenn's during his playing days, and the amiable hitting coach encouraged him not to change it, no matter what anyone else said.

"Maybe he saw that and took a liking to me," said Yount. "I didn't know much about him as a player, except for his name. He was always talking to me, from the very beginning, talking hitting. I became very close to Harvey and Audrey."

Kuenn had a tough side, too, and wasn't opposed to chewing out a player he thought was doing things the wrong way, on or off the field. But, more often than not, he was the players' friend, offering a pat on the butt or a kind word at the appropriate times.

"He taught me how to play the game, basically," Yount said. "It was more than just the hitting of a baseball. He was a play-hard-all-the-time type guy, which was how I felt the game was supposed to be played, too. Whenever he said something, I took it to heart. If he said this was the way something was supposed to be done, in my opinion that was the way it was supposed to be done. That's how much I respected him."

Kuenn also earned the respect of players by not letting the series of serious health setbacks get him down. He never complained, never asked "Why me?" His toughness rubbed off on what became a team of rugged veterans who didn't let nagging injuries get in the way of their jobs, if they could help it.

"You could never tell whether he was having a good day or a bad day," said Yount. "He was always the same guy, and a very successful one at that, and one I respected immensely."

General Manager Harry Dalton couldn't help noticing the tight bond between Kuenn and the players. Two months into the '82 season, when Dalton concluded that manager Buck Rodgers was not the right man to get the job done, he didn't look far for a successor. Dalton told team owner Bud Selig he thought it was time to replace Rodgers with Kuenn. Selig immediately agreed.

"Harvey was a perfect match," said Selig. "We had a talented team, a veteran club that knew how to play, with great competitors. They just needed to be allowed to play. Buck was more hands-on. He was a good baseball man, but

Harvey just let them play."

"He told us to do the things you need to do to win baseball games," added Caldwell. "'Go out and play hard from the time you get here until the time you go home. That's all I can ask.' It was that simple. And baseball really is a simple game. He put the lineup up there, made a few moves at the right time and sat back and watched us play. He treated us all like we were his No. 1 son."

No one associated with the club thought it was a coincidence that the Brewers took off under the understated guidance of Kuenn. When he took over as manager on June 2, Milwaukee was 23-24 and in fifth place in the AL East. By the time the smoke cleared in Baltimore on the last day of the season, the Brewers had gone 72-43 with Kuenn at the helm, finishing with the best record in the major leagues, and clinking the division.

A team loaded with big boppers quickly earned the fabulously appropriate nickname "Harvey's Wallbangers." Kuenn was named AL manager of the year, but what his players would tell you is that he primarily stayed out of the way.

"I remember Harvey's first meeting," said Don Money, a veteran infielder-turned-DH on the '82 club. "It was a very short meeting. He told us, 'Get rid of all of the trick plays. You can try to pick guys off, but do it yourself. We don't have to have a sign.'

"Buck put a lot of plays on. He liked doing it himself. Harvey let us do it ourselves. There was a little friction between Buck and a couple of older players. They just didn't see eye to eye. When Harvey took over, we got it going."

Most of the players referred to Kuenn as "Arch," though to this day none of them can tell you the origin of that name. Longtime Brewers radio announcer Bob Uecker solved the mystery, noting it was given Kuenn by former Detroit teammate Billy Hoeft.

"Billy Hoeft called him that because he thought he looked like Archie from the comic books," explained Uecker. "Billy was from Wisconsin, too, and they were very close friends. That's what all of us called him. Arch."

Kuenn looked the other way each afternoon as a majority of his players gathered in a circle in a corner of the field, hours before game time, and played "flip," a playful yet fierce competition in which they batted a baseball at each other with their gloves. If you couldn't keep it in play, you were out. Because of the inherent dangers of balls flying toward the faces of players, Dalton mulled putting an end to the "flip" games. Kuenn talked him out of it, insisting it helped build the camaraderie that all winning teams have.

"Guys would get it off the lip, off the chin," recalled first baseman Cecil Cooper. "It might be heated for a minute, but then it was gone. It was part of it. If you got a fat lip, you kept playing. You don't see that anymore. You don't have the togetherness today like we had back then. You learned from each other back then, talking about the game and all that. Harvey understood that."

October was a bittersweet month for the Brewers under Kuenn. They won the AL East in dramatic fashion on the final day of the season in Baltimore, then roared back from a 0-2 hole in the ALCS to topple California for the pennant. As high as the Brewers were at that point, it all came crashing down in a heartbreaking seven-game defeat to St. Louis in the World Series.

Kuenn kept the Brewers in the pennant race again in 1983 until late August. A West Coast swing to Oakland, Seattle and California, during which the club stumbled with a 3-6 record, proved to be its undoing. The Brewers went from a half-game up to five behind on that trip and never recovered. Injuries and age were starting to take their toll, and Dalton sensed a time of change was coming. In a painful decision, he made Kuenn part of that change, replacing him the day after the season ended with former Seattle manager Rene Lachemann.

Kuenn remained connected to the Brewers, serving as a scout and consultant to Dalton. Eventually, he and Audrey did what many Wisconsinites their age did — move to the Phoenix area. It was in his home there on February 28, 1988, that Kuenn died of a heart attack at 57. The news deeply saddened those who played for him that marvelous summer when "Harvey's Wallbangers" captured the hearts of baseball fans in Milwaukee and the entire state.

"It was like losing a family member," said Yount. "That's how close we had become."

Among the players who served as pallbearers at Kuenn's funeral was former Cy Young Award winner Pete Vuckovich, whose gruff exterior cracked under the raw emotion of having to bury his beloved manager at too young of an age.

"I helped carry him to his grave," said Vuckovich. "I cried that day and I'm not ashamed to admit it. I loved Harvey."

For those who knew him, it was impossible to feel otherwise.

THE ARCHITECT

In the mid to late '70s, the Brewers were slowly but surely building a powerful club. They had drafted well, and home-grown players such as Robin Yount, Paul Molitor, Jim Gantner, Gorman Thomas and Moose Haas were making their presence known.

To get over the top, however, the Brewers needed help from the outside. That's where Harry Dalton came in. Hired on November 20, 1977, by team president Bud Selig to oversee the final stages of the club's transition from perennial loser to pennant contender, Dalton showed a deft touch for making the right move at the right time.

He was known primarily for making the blockbuster trade at the winter meetings in 1980 that netted a pair of future Cy Young Award winners Pete Vuckovich and Rollie Fingers as well as all-star catcher Ted Simmons. And, certainly, that deal was greatly responsible for pushing the team into the spotlight of October competition.

But Dalton made other astute moves that proved just as important in leading the Brewers' to their first and only World Series appearance.

"Harry did a fantastic job," said Haas. "He wasn't afraid to make moves. I don't know how he made those deals, but he did."

A couple of key acquisitions were made before Dalton's arrival. It was Selig who orchestrated the trade with Boston at the winter meetings in 1976 that brought first baseman Cecil Cooper to the Brewers in exchange for George "Boomer" Scott and Bernie Carbo. Cooper evolved into one of the best hitters in the American League and delivered the pennant-winning two-run single in the 1982 ALCS comeback triumph over California.

"That was my only trade," recalled Selig. "Even the great Branch Rickey couldn't have done better than that, so I quit while I was ahead."

In another move that proved to be a steal, left-hander Mike Caldwell was acquired from Cincinnati in June 1977 for minor leaguers Rick O'Keefe and Gary Pyka. O'Keefe, a right-handed pitcher, was the Brewers' first-round draft pick in 1975 but never played a day in the big leagues. Neither did Pyka.

Two days before Dalton was hired, the Brewers signed free agent outfielder Larry Hisle, an offensive force whose time in Milwaukee unfortunately was cut short by a shoulder injury a few years later. The day before Hisle joined the fold, veteran third baseman Sal Bando signed a free-agent deal.

Key players such as third baseman Don Money and reliever Bob McClure were obtained in trades in previous years. But Dalton left no stone unturned in adding more players. He filled out his roster by plucking reserve outfielders Mark Brouhard and Marshall Edwards as well as backup catcher Ned Yost from other teams in the Rule 5 winter draft.

Dalton pulled off a slick bit of maneuvering by trading right-hander Jim Slaton to Detroit in December 1977 for outfielder Ben Oglivie, who eventually replaced the injured Hisle, then re-signing Slaton as a free agent after the '78 season. Slaton went on to become the franchise's all-time leader in victories.

Thomas, a fan favorite who was traded to Texas a month before Dalton's arrival, was reacquired by the new GM before the start of the next season.

"A lot of the pieces were here already, but Harry did great adding the finishing touches," said Selig. "He made some great moves."

The greatest of all came at the winter meetings in 1980, when he acquired Vuckovich, Fingers and Simmons in a stunning seven-player swap with St. Louis that transformed the Brewers into an immediate playoff team. Dalton later admitted it was a trade that almost never happened.

It was Dalton, not St. Louis general manager/manager Whitey Herzog, who threatened to call off the proposed deal. He knew Fingers was available because the Cardinals had closer Bruce Sutter but didn't want to trade outfield prospect David Green, whom Herzog coveted.

"He was on the list of people we wouldn't trade," Dalton said in a Milwaukee *Journal Sentinel* interview five years ago. "The last several hours, we were still saying no."

Finally, Dalton decided to concentrate on today and worry about tomorrow later. Fingers, Vuckovich and Simmons would make the Brewers a serious contender now. Green might or might not pan out (as it turned out, he didn't). Dalton also sent popular outfielder Sixto Lezcano to the Cardinals as well as pitchers Larry Sorensen and Dave LaPoint. It was a trade he never regretted making.

Fingers led the majors with 28 saves during the strike-split '81 season, becoming the first pitcher to win the AL Cy Young and MVP Award in the same season. The Brewers advanced to the playoffs for the first time in franchise history, bowing to the powerful New York Yankees in the mini-playoffs.

"We didn't have a closer until we got Rollie," said Gantner. "That was an unbelievable trade. If we had a closer like Rollie in '78, '79 and '80, there would have been no stopping us. Harry got a lot of pitchers in trades. He did a great job. It seemed like everything he did was right."

As the '82 season progressed, Dalton decided his pitching rotation needed some help. Left-hander Randy Lerch was 8-7 through 20 starts but was scuffling with a 4.97 ERA. On August 11, Dalton purchased veteran right-hander Doc Medich from Texas. Three days later, Lerch was sold to the Montreal Expos.

But Dalton's signature move came on August 30, one day before the deadline for players to remain eligible for post-season play. Dalton picked up future Hall of Fame pitcher Don Sutton from Houston for three players to be named later, who turned out to be young outfielder Kevin Bass and pitchers Frank DiPino and Mike Madden.

Without Sutton, the Brewers would have been spectators in the post-season, not participants. The crafty right-hander went 4-1 with a 3.29 ERA in seven starts and won the biggest regular-season game in franchise history on the final day of the season in Baltimore, preventing a monumental collapse by the Brewers. That victory alone made the price worthwhile for acquiring Sutton, who proved to be the proverbial last piece to the puzzle.

"When [Dalton] traded for Sutton, that was the first time we picked up somebody in late August that made a difference on our ball club," said Gantner.

Just as important as the player moves Dalton made over the years were two managerial hires. Shortly after taking over as general manager, he targeted long-time Baltimore pitching coach George Bamberger as the man to lead the Brewers to the playoffs. Dalton knew Bamberger from their days together with the Orioles, who captured four pennants and two World Series during his tenure as vice president of player personnel.

First, Dalton had to convince Selig that Bamberger was the right man for the job. He set up a dinner meeting at the University Club in Milwaukee, where the conversation began in startling fashion.

As Selig took his seat, he said to Bamberger, "George, nice to meet you. I hope you're going to come with us."

To which Bamberger replied, "You're a bunch of losers. Why would I want to come here?"

It was typical Bamberger, a salty, straight-talking man who called them as he saw them. By the end of the evening, everybody was laughing, and Bamberger was the Brewers' new skipper. The ball club, soon dubbed "Bambi's Bombers," went from 67 victories to 93 in his first year at the helm. The Brewers followed with a 95-victory season, but Bamberger suffered a slight heart attack in 1980 and eventually stepped aside in favor of Buck Rodgers.

"I really think that was the turnabout for the franchise, when Bambi was hired," said Selig. "It was sad when he got sick. He was my favorite. I loved him. He used to kid that he taught me how to swear, which wasn't true."

Dalton's other sage managerial move came two months into the '82 season, when a potent Brewers club was spinning its wheels under the hands-on approach of Rodgers. Realizing the veteran-laden team needed a lighter grip on the reins, he moved hitting coach Harvey Kuenn into the manager's office and the Brewers took off. There was no stopping "Harvey's Wallbangers."

"We started building from '78 on," said Don Money, a dependable third baseman who joined the club in 1973 and played for the Brewers for 11 years. "We won a lot of games in those next few years, but some other club always won more. That was a tough division. We just didn't have enough pieces in the late '70's to finish first. The trade Harry made with St. Louis finally put us over the hump."

It's a general manager's job to build a winning club, but it's also his duty to know when to tear it apart and start over. After the Brewers faded down the stretch in '83 and fell out of the running, Dalton began deconstructing his injury-plagued and aging club. There were some decent seasons in the late '80s under manager Tom Trebelhorn, but the Brewers never made it back to the playoffs.

After the 1991 season, in what he called "the most difficult decision I ever made," Selig pushed Dalton aside in favor of Bando, who had been an advisor to both men. Dalton claimed Selig "never told me a reason" for the move, but the game was changing, and the way Dalton saw it, not for the better.

After a few years in a consultant role with the club, Dalton retired to his home in Carefree, Arizona. He contracted Parkinson's disease not long after, and died in 2005, two years after being inducted into the Brewers' Walk of Fame at Miller Park. Many of the players he acquired to get the Brewers to the '82 World Series attended his funeral.

In Dalton's 15 years running the Brewers' baseball operation, the team had nine winning seasons. With the players he put in place, the Brewers went 92-70 in 1992, the year after he was dismissed. They haven't had a winning season since.

THE BOSS

It was something Bud Selig never had done before as owner of the Brewers, and something he never did again.

On October 3, 1982, Selig had this gnawing feeling that he should address his players before they took the field at Baltimore's Memorial Stadium. The stunned Brewers had lost the first three games of the season-ending series, and in truly ugly fashion, by a combined score of 26-7.

"We got slaughtered," said Selig.

The night before, Selig had not slept. He paced back and forth in the courtyard of the team hotel, smoking one Tiparillo after another. Selig went back to his room and watched *The Dirty Dozen*, not once, but twice. Finally, at 7 a.m., he dozed off, only to be awakened an hour and half later by a knock at the door.

"What did you order room service for?" Selig asked his wife, Sue. "We're not going to the ballpark until 2 o'clock."

"I didn't order room service," she replied, sleepily.

Selig opened the door and in barged Howard Cosell, the mouth that roared, uninvited yet undeterred. Cosell would be broadcasting the division-deciding game that afternoon and wanted to pick Selig's brain as to the mood of his club. Selig ordered breakfast and the two sat down to chat.

"You're going to win today," Cosell told Selig. "I've known (starting pitcher) Don Sutton for years."

After Cosell departed, Selig peeked out his hotel window and sure enough, there were Sutton and catcher Ted Simmons, sitting on a bench, going over the Baltimore hitters. Thinking back to Cosell's words of encouragement, his mood brightened. It was a month or so later that Orioles owner Edward Bennett Williams informed Selig that Cosell had dropped by to visit him that morning, too, predicting his club was in great shape with Jim Palmer on the mound.

"I told him my story about Howard," said Selig. "He says, 'That son of a bitch.' So, Edward grabs the phone and calls Howard. His wife, Emmy, answers and he said, 'Let me talk to Howard.' He swears at him and then hands me the phone. I said, 'Howard, what were you doing?' He said, 'What are you guys mad at me for? I made you both feel good.'"

But not good enough. When Selig got to the ballpark, he asked general manager Harry Dalton and manager Harvey Kuenn if it would be appropriate for him to address the players before the game. Selig didn't want to put any more pressure on a team that had blown a three-game lead in three days but couldn't fight back the urge to voice his support.

"To say I was nervous would be the understatement of the century," he recalled.

Selig stepped into the cramped visitors' clubhouse. A hush fell over the players as they sat in front of their lockers.

"Look, guys, I know this has been tough," said Selig. "But I'm proud of you and I love all of you for your effort. I'm proud to be associated with you. Just go do the best you can, and you'll always have my support."

Selig turned and walked out of the clubhouse, praying he had set the right tone for his club.

"That's the only time I ever talked to the players before a game," he said.

Whether Selig's words made any difference, he'll never know. But the Brewers went out and played like a team without a care in the world. They pounded the Orioles and Palmer, 10-2, behind two early home runs by Robin Yount, finally pulling away with five runs in the ninth to capture their first AL East crown.

Sitting in the box seats near the Milwaukee dugout, Selig could barely contain himself. Afraid to let himself believe it was actually happening, he sat back and breathed a huge sigh of relief after the ninth-inning outburst.

"I can still close my eyes and see Ted Simmons' home run go into the left-field bleachers," recalled Selig. "I thought, 'Oh, my God, we're going to win.'"

Breaking free from the raucous clubhouse celebration afterward, first baseman Cecil Cooper brought a bottle of champagne out to the Seligs, allowing them to toast the victory.

Asked to express his feelings that day, Selig said, "It was relief and genuine happiness. People don't understand how tough it is to win in baseball. People have forgotten how good that team was for all those years. Harry always thought we didn't get enough credit. We were in a really tough division and there was no wild card."

It was on to California and the American League Championship Series against the Angels. Before they knew what hit them, the Brewers had lost the first two games, falling into a hole from which no club had escaped in the best-of-five format. Selig was left to wonder if it was the Brewers' fate never to experience the thrills of a World Series.

"You finally get in the playoffs and, bang, before you know it, you're down 0-2," he said. "And not a good 0-2. I think the guys were exhausted and a little tight."

Selig's spirits lifted when the Brewers returned home to County Stadium and pulled out Game 3, 5-3, behind another clutch performance by Sutton. His club was still alive but the weather turned ugly the next day, as it so often does in Milwaukee that time of year, and Selig didn't want to play the game.

"This is crazy," he told commissioner Bowie Kuhn. "Don't play. It's rainy and cold."

Smelling the kill, Angels president Lee MacPhail also was bending Kuhn's ear, telling him the game should go on. A firm believer that post-season games should be played if at all possible, Kuhn told Selig there would be no postponement. Years later, when Selig became commissioner, he came to appreciate Kuhn's point of view on the subject.

Behind a huge offensive display by Mark Brouhard, normally a backup outfielder, the Brewers pounded the Angels, 9-5, to draw even and put the pennant up for grabs. Leaving the stadium, Selig bumped into his counterpart.

"Are you still mad we played now?" said the agitated MacPhail, who stormed off in a huff.

The next day, the weather was better, but not by much. Though his team had all the momentum at that point, Selig stayed true to his nervous nature, wearing out yet another pair of shoes and going through box after box of Tiparillos. Looking for any good luck charm he could find, Selig insisted that Hall of Famer Don Drysdale, a Chicago White Sox broadcaster who had dropped in for Game 3, stay through the weekend. Chicago owner Jerry Reinsdorf called that morning, informing Selig that Drysdale was supposed to be working with pitchers at the team's instructional camp.

"Too bad," said Selig. "He's not going. I'm keeping him."

Earl Weaver, who announced his retirement after the Orioles lost to the Brewers on that final day in Baltimore (he'd return briefly in 1985), was a guest analyst on the telecast of the game. He asked Selig if his wife, Marianna, could sit in the owner's box. Selig said fine, knowing full well his own wife would not sit there during games because her husband couldn't control his temper or language.

Thanks to Cooper's clutch two-run single in the seventh, the Brewers took a 4-3 lead into the top of the ninth. Ron Jackson opened with a single off reliever Bob McClure, and Kuenn summoned rookie Pete Ladd, who had filled in admirably over the final weeks of the season for injured closer Rollie Fingers. Bob Boone bunted pinch-runner Rob Wilfong to second, and he remained there

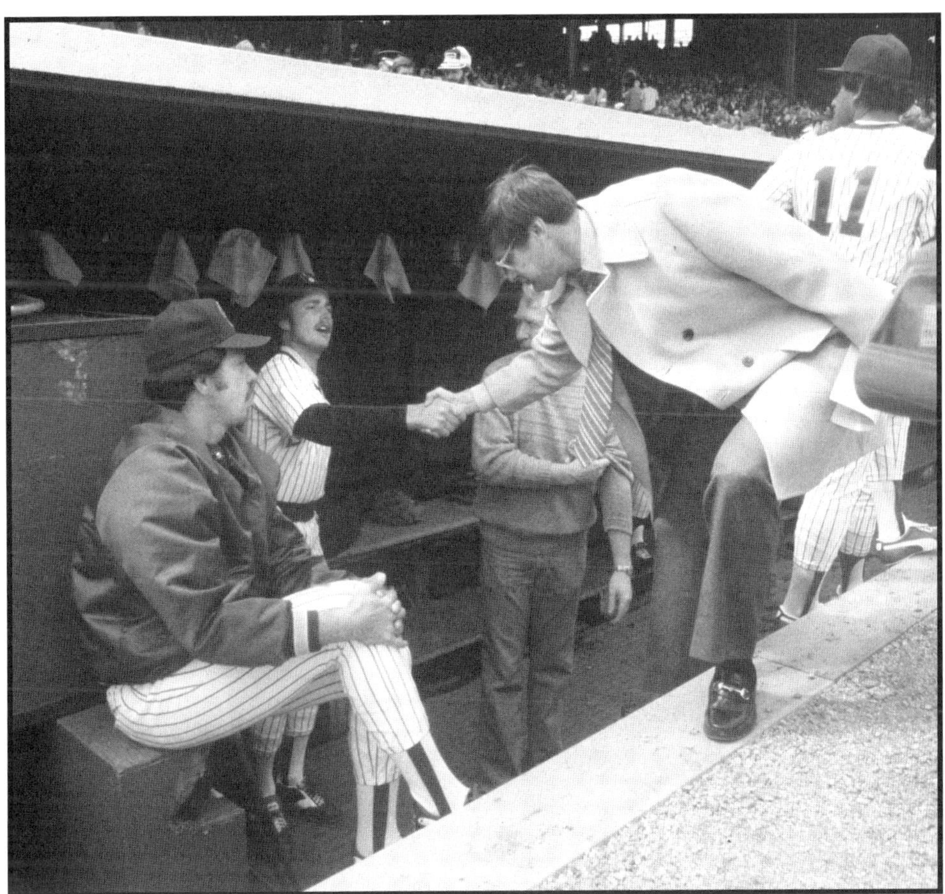

Selig wishes Jim Gantner good luck prior to the start of Game 5 in the '82 World Series.

as Brian Downing grounded out to third baseman Paul Molitor.

With his team one out away from a berth in the World Series, Selig closed his eyes. When he opened them to watch the next California hitter settle into the batter's box, his spirits sunk.

"I hated ninth innings," he said. "I hate them to this day, and I don't have a team anymore. I look down and here's Rod Carew coming to the plate. I'm up in my box, smoking one Tiparillo with another lit one in the ash tray. Smoke is going everywhere. How Marianna Weaver stood it, I'll never know.

"I said out loud, 'After all these years, why does it have to be Rod Carew? Why can't it be somebody who can't hit? No, it has to be the great Rod Carew.'"

And, sure enough, Carew hit Ladd's pitch on the nose. But it zipped on one hop right to shortstop Robin Yount, who threw over to Cooper for the pennant-clinching out. In an instant, the players were engulfed by a sea of humanity. The Brewers were going to the World Series!

Getting pats on the back and hearty handshakes from those around him, Selig was trembling. He fought the urge to run down and celebrate with the players. Instead, he walked down the ramps to his tiny office, closed the door behind him and sat down, tears streaming down his face.

"I just wanted to soak it in," he said. "You could hear the crowd outside going wild."

When Selig drove home around 9 o'clock that night, the streets were still filled with cheering, celebrating fans, many honking their car horns. He still had trouble believing it was real, but it hit him squarely later that evening sitting in his den, reading the Sunday paper. He had tuned his radio to the CBS station and was listening to the national news when it came time for the sports segment.

Selig heard the voice say, "The teams for the 79th World Series are set. It's the Milwaukee Brewers and the St. Louis Cardinals."

Yes, it was really happening. Selig started crying, again.

The World Series got off to a magnificent start for Selig's team. The Brewers pounded the Cardinals, 10-0, in Game 1 behind a masterful pitching performance by veteran lefty Mike Caldwell. But the long-awaited moment was tainted by a family tragedy. Walking to the game from a nearby hotel, Selig's mother, Marie, fell and broke her hip.

It was Marie Selig who introduced her son to the game of baseball as a small boy, taking him on exciting trips to New York and Chicago on the train. He had visited Yankee Stadium, the Polo Grounds, Dodger Stadium, Wrigley Field, Comiskey Park. No young, eager baseball fan could have asked for more.

"She had looked forward to the Brewers getting to the World Series so much," he recalled. "We went to the hospital after the game that night and she said, 'I'm not doing so well, but the Brewers are doing great.' We brought her back to Milwaukee on the team plane after Game 2, but she never got to go to a game. It was something I always regretted."

When the Brewers won two of three games in Milwaukee to take a 3-2 lead in the Series, Selig tried to convince himself it was meant to be, that the Brewers were destined to be champions. Like everyone else associated with the club, he was devastated when the Cardinals won the last two games at home to earn the coveted trophy.

To this day, Selig believes the Brewers would have won it all if not for the injury to Fingers, who didn't pitch after Labor Day. The Cardinals had their wonderful closer, Bruce Sutter, who finished off the Brewers with two scoreless innings in Game 7.

"I had a lot of faith in that club," he said. "I knew the Cardinals were good, don't get me wrong, but I thought we were better. Rollie was such a great pitcher. In '81, he was unhittable. He was unhittable in '82, also, and all of a sudden we don't have him. Pete Ladd did a very admirable job, I'll say that, but he wasn't Rollie Fingers. Nobody was."

One of Selig's favorite tasks as commissioner is placing a congratulatory telephone call each year to the players elected to the Hall of Fame. In 2006, he dutifully placed his call to Sutter, the only player chosen.

"When I called him, he said, 'Are you still mad at me?'" recalled Selig. "I said, 'No.' He said, 'Remember, they had me. You guys didn't have Fingers.'"

When the Brewers returned home from St. Louis after the devastating Game 7 defeat, Selig initially fought the city's plans to hold a parade for the team.

"Are they nuts?" Selig asked club vice president Dick Hackett. "We lost. Nobody's going to be there. I'm not doing it."

Hackett and Sue Selig eventually talked the distraught owner into it, and it turned out to be a day he'll never forget. With the streets filled with cheering, adoring fans, you never would have known the Brewers had lost the Series. The ceremonies were capped by a raucous celebration at County Stadium, during which Yount thrilled all in attendance — except a frightened Selig - by roaring onto the field on his motorcycle.

"I almost had a heart attack," said Selig. "But it was great."

There were many lean years afterward for the Brewers, much to the chagrin of Selig. He eventually moved on to his role as commissioner and later sold the team. But he'll always cherish that unforgettable 1982 season, when "Harvey's Wallbangers" captured the imagination of baseball fans throughout Wisconsin, earning a permanent place in their hearts.

"It was really a team for the ages," said Selig. "I'm immensely proud of all of them. I regarded them like my own family. You don't have that anymore. The love that the city and state had for that team was really unbelievable. I don't think you'll ever see that again."

More Great Titles From KCI Sports!

Green and Golden Moments
Bob Harlan and the Green Bay Packers
6 x 9 Hardcover 280pp $24.95

In his autobiography—*Green and Golden Moments*—Harlan invites Packers fans to reminisce with him about the highs and lows of a career spent in sports. From his time at Marquette University with legendary coach Al McGuire to winning a World Championship with Stan Musial and the St. Louis Cardinals to his 36 years with the Green & Gold, Harlan shares his stories and offers a behind-the-scenes look at one of the greatest franchises in professional sports: the Green Bay Packers.

This is the story of how a kid from Iowa who wanted to be a sports writer built a career, in his own low key, unassuming way, as one of the most effective executives in any game in America.

DON'T FLINCH
Barry Alvarez: The Autobiography
6 x 9 Hardcover 280pp $24.95

Despite inheriting a moribund college football program, and half-empty stadium, Barry Alvarez never compromised his values, never flinched — even after a 1-10 first season — and never stopped believing in his blue print for success at the University of Wisconsin.

In his autobiography — *Don't Flinch* — Alvarez talks about the lessons that he learned from his exposure to three legendary coaches, Nebraska's Bob Devaney, Iowa's Hayden Fry and Notre Dame's Lou Holtz, the hurdles that he had to overcome as a young assistant and high school coach, and the challenge of taking over his own college program. By establishing a solid foundation, adhering to fundamentals and demanding an uncommon toughness from his players, Alvarez became the architect of three Rose Bowl triumphs in the '90s and became the school's all-time winningest football coach. Alvarez maps out a strategy and game plan for young coaches who are seeking to achieve similar goals, and he also talks about his future as Wisconsin athletics director, and the future of college football.

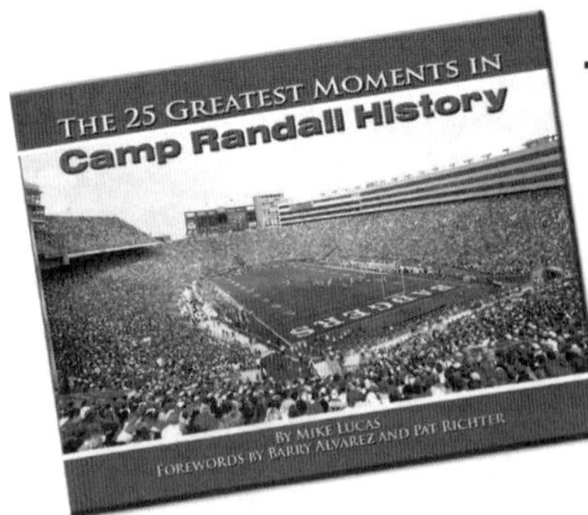

The 25 Greatest Moments in Camp Randall History
12 x 9 Hardcover 160pp $24.95

Throughout the years the University of Wisconsin football program has provided Badger fans with many memorable moments at Camp Randall Stadium: the running of Heisman Trophy winners Alan "The Horse" Ameche and Ron "The Great" Dayne; the rough-and-tumble days of the '51 Hard Rocks; '42 legends like Elroy "Crazy Legs" Hirsch and Dave Schreiner; the Matt Schabert-to-Lee Evans touchdown pass to beat #3-ranked Ohio State in '03; and the '81 upset of #1-ranked Michigan. Which moment is the most memorable? Let the great debate begin.

Available at your local bookstore or by calling KCI Sports at 1-800-697-3756